A WORLD OF THREE ZEROS

Also by Muhammad Yunus:
  Banker to the Poor
  Creating a World Without Poverty
  Building Social Business

A WORLD *of* THREE ZEROS

THE NEW ECONOMICS *of*
ZERO POVERTY,
ZERO UNEMPLOYMENT,
and ZERO NET CARBON EMISSIONS

MUHAMMAD YUNUS

with KARL WEBER

PUBLICAFFAIRS

New York

The Hachette Speakers Bureau provides a wide range of authors for speaking events. To find out more, go to hachettespeakersbureau.com or call 866-376-6591.

Book Design by Amy Quinn

Library of Congress Cataloging-in-Publication Data

Names: Yunus, Muhammad, 1940- author. | Weber, Karl, 1953- author. Title: A world of three zeros : the new economics of zero poverty, zero unemployment, and zero carbon emissions / Muhammad Yunus, with Karl Weber. Description: First edition. | New York : PublicAffairs, [2017] | Includes bibliographical references and index. Identifiers: LCCN 2017017988 | ISBN 9781610397575 (hardcover) Subjects: LCSH: Social responsibility of business. | Capitalism—Social aspects. | Economic development—Social aspects. | Sustainable development. | Equality—Economic aspects. Classification: LCC HD60 .Y863 2017 | DDC 330—dc23LC record available at https://lccn.loc.gov/2017017988

ISBNs: 978-1-61039-757-5 (HC); 978-1-61039-758-2 (EB); 978-1-5417-6792-8 (INTL)

First Edition

LSC-C

10 9 8 7 6 5 4 3 2 1

To the young generation,
who will build a new civilization

CONTENTS

PART

ONE

THE CHALLENGE

1

THE FAILURES OF CAPITALISM

I'VE DEVOTED MOST OF MY life to working for the poorest people, particularly the poorest women, trying to remove the hurdles they face in their efforts to improve their lives. Through the tool known as microcredit, Grameen Bank, which I launched in my home country of Bangladesh in 1976, makes capital available to poor villagers, especially women. Microcredit has since unleashed the entrepreneurial capabilities of over 300 million poor people around the world, helping to break the chains of poverty and exploitation that have enslaved them.

The impact of microcredit in enabling millions of people to lift themselves out of poverty helped to expose the shortcomings of a traditional banking system that denied its services to those who needed them most—the world's poorest people. This is just one of many interrelated problems suffered by the poor: lack of institutional services, lack of clean drinking water and sanitary facilities, lack of health care, inadequate education, substandard housing, no access to energy, neglect in old age, and many more. And these problems are not restricted to the developing world. In my global travels, I've found that low-income people in the world's richest nations are suffering from many of the same problems. In the words of Angus Deaton, a Nobel Prize–winning economist, "If you had to choose between living in a poor village in India and living in the Mississippi Delta or in a suburb of Milwaukee in a trailer park, I'm not sure who would have the better life."[1]

The Rising Tide of Wealth Concentration

THE TROUBLES PLAGUING POOR PEOPLE throughout the world reflect an even broader economic and social problem— the problem of rising inequality caused by continuous wealth concentration.

Inequality has been a hot subject in politics for ages. Many powerful political and social movements and many ambitious initiatives have been launched in recent years that attempt to address this problem. Much blood has been shed over the issue. But the problem is as far from being solved as ever. In fact, plenty of evidence shows that, in recent decades, the problem of the ever-expanding gap in individual wealth has been getting worse. As the economy grows, so does the concentration of wealth. This trend has continued and even accelerated despite the positive effects of national and international development programs, income redistribution programs, and other efforts to alleviate the problems of low-income people. Microcredit and other programs have helped many lift themselves out of poverty, but at the same time the richest have continued to claim a greater share of the world's wealth.

The trend toward ever-increasing wealth concentration is dangerous because it threatens human progress, social cohesion, human rights, and democracy. A world in which wealth is concentrated in a few hands is also a world in which political power is controlled by a few and used by them for their own benefit.

As wealth concentration increases within countries, it also increases between nations. So even as millions of poor people work to lift themselves out of poverty, the bulk of the world's wealth continues to be concentrated in half a dozen countries.

As the wealth gap and the power gap grow, mistrust, resentment, and anger inevitably deepen, pushing the world toward social upheaval and increasing the likelihood of armed conflicts among nations.

Oxfam is an international confederation of eighteen nonprofit organizations that are focused on the alleviation of global poverty. Experts at Oxfam have been studying the problem of increasing wealth concentration. The data they have uncovered are truly horrifying.

In 2010, Oxfam reported that the world's richest 388 people owned more wealth than the entire bottom half of the world population—a group that included an estimated 3.3 billion human beings. At the time, this was considered a startling statistic, and it was reported as such around the world. But in the years since then, the problem has grown much worse. In January 2017, Oxfam announced that the ultraprivileged group that owns wealth exceeding that of the bottom half of the world's population has shrunk to just eight people—even as the number of people in the bottom half has grown to about 3.6 billion.[2] Newspapers published the pictures of these eight people. They are well-known, well-respected people—American business leaders like Bill Gates, Warren Buffett, and Jeff Bezos, as well as a few from other countries, such as Amancio Ortega of Spain and Carlos Slim Helú of Mexico.

This information is so unbelievable that it takes time to absorb. We feel like asking many more questions. What happens to the social fabric in a country where a handful of people control the bulk of the national wealth? When we get to the point where one person controls a huge portion of a country's wealth, what is to prevent that person from imposing his will on the nation? Implicitly or explicitly, his wishes will become the law of the land.

It could easily happen in a low-income country like Bangladesh. But we now realize it can also happen in a wealthy country like the United States. In his 2016 presidential campaign, Senator Bernie Sanders frequently pointed out that the richest 0.1 percent of Americans own as much wealth as the bottom 90 percent—a claim supported by solid research data from sources like the nonpartisan National Bureau of Economic Research.[3] He also pointed out that the Walton family of Walmart has more wealth than the bottom 40 percent of the US population—another claim that research by unbiased fact-checkers has supported.[4]

It is dangerous for a country to allow so much wealth and power to be concentrated in a few hands. Perhaps it's not surprising that the US presidential race ended with the election of a man with practically no credentials as a national leader other than his vast personal wealth.

HOW CAPITALISM BREEDS INEQUALITY

MANY SPECIFIC FEATURES OF TODAY'S financial and political landscape have contributed to the problem of wealth concentration. But the basic reality is that wealth concentration is an all-but-inevitable, nonstop process under the present economic system. Contrary to one popular belief, the richest people are not necessarily evil manipulators who have rigged the system through bribery or corruption. In reality, the current capitalist system works on their behalf. Wealth acts like a magnet. The biggest magnet naturally draws smaller magnets toward it. That's how the present economic system is built. And most people give this system their tacit support. People envy the very rich, but they usually don't attack them. Young children are encouraged to try to become wealthy themselves when they grow up.

By contrast, poor people—people with no magnet—find it difficult to attract anything to them. If they somehow manage to acquire a tiny magnet of their own, retaining it is difficult. The bigger magnets exert an almost irresistible attraction. Unidirectional forces of concentration keep changing the shape of the wealth graph, making it a wall rising to the sky at the highest percentile of the wealth scale while the columns for the rest of the population barely rise above the ground.

Such a structure is unsustainable. Socially and politically, it is a ticking time bomb, waiting to destroy everything we have created over the years. Yet this is the frightening reality that has taken shape around us while we were busy with our daily lives, ignoring the writing on the wall.

This is not what the promoters of the traditional vision of capitalism taught us to expect. Since the appearance of modern capitalism some 250 years ago, the concept of the free market as a natural regulator of wealth has come to be widely accepted. Many of us have been taught that an "invisible hand" ensures competition in the economy, contributing to equilibrium in the markets and generating social benefits that are automatically shared by everyone. Free markets dedicated solely to profit are supposed to produce improved living standards for all.

Capitalism has indeed stimulated innovation and economic growth. But in a world of skyrocketing inequality, more and more people are asking, "Does the invisible hand produce its benefits for everybody in the society?" The answer seems obvious. Somehow the invisible hand must be heavily biased toward the richest—otherwise, how could today's enormous wealth concentration continue to grow?

Many of us were raised to believe in the slogan "Economic growth is a rising tide that lifts all boats." The saying ignores the plight of the millions who are clinging to leaky rafts—or who have no boats at all.

In his best-selling book *Capital in the Twenty-First Century* (Harvard University Press, 2014), economist Thomas Piketty provided an exhaustive analysis of the tendency of contemporary capitalism to increase economic inequality. His diagnosis of the problem stimulated debate around the world. Piketty was fundamentally correct about the nature of the problem. But his proposed solution, which relies mainly on the use of progressive taxation to remedy income imbalances, was not equal to the task.

A more fundamental change in the way we think about economics is necessary. It's time to admit that the neoclassical vision of capitalism offers no solution to the economic problems we face. It has produced amazing technological advances and huge accumulations of wealth but at the cost of creating massive inequality and the terrible human problems that inequality fosters. We need to abandon our unquestioning faith in the power of personal-profit-centered markets to solve all problems and confess that the problems of inequality are not going to be solved by the natural workings of the economy as it is currently structured. Rather, the problems will become more and more acute very fast.

This is not just a problem that affects the "losers" in the game of capitalist competition—who in fact are the over- whelming majority of the world's population. It impacts the national and global social and political environment, eco- nomic progress, and quality of life for all of us—including those in the wealthy minority.

The rise of inequality has led to social unrest, political po- larization, and growing tensions among groups. It underlay phenomena as varied as the Occupy movement, the Tea Party, and the Arab Spring; the passage of Brexit in the United King- dom; the election of Donald Trump; and the rise of right-wing nationalism, racism, and hate groups in Europe and the United States. People who feel disinherited and left without prospects for the future have become increasingly disenchanted and an- gry. Our world has become sharply divided between the haves and the have-nots—two groups with little in common except a mutual sense of distrust, fear, and hostility. This distrust will only become more pronounced as information and communi- cation technologies continue to spread among the bottommost segment of the population, making them even more aware of how unfairly the cards have been stacked against them.

This is not a comfortable situation for anyone, including those who are on top of the social heap at any given time. Do the wealthy and powerful enjoy life behind the bars of gated communities, hiding from the realities of existence as the 99 percent experience it? Do they like having to avert their eyes from the homeless and hungry people they pass on the street? Do they enjoy using the tools of the state—including its police powers and other forms of coercion—to suppress the inevitable protests mounted by those on the bottom? Do they really want their own children and grandchildren to inherit this kind of world?

I think that for most wealthy people, the answer is no.

I don't think rich people became rich because they are bad people. Many of them are good people who simply made use of the existing economic system to reach the top of the ladder. And many of them share the widespread feeling of uneasiness over living in a world that is sharply divided between rich and poor.

One piece of evidence is the large sums of money that people donate to charitable causes, either in the form of individual gifts to nonprofit organizations or through philanthropic foundations. People give away hundreds of billions of dollars to charities every year. Even most corporations, while their leaders may pay allegiance to the doctrine that profit maximization is the only valid function of business, siphon off a percentage of their profits to community service projects and charitable gifts in the name of "social responsibility."

Furthermore, practically every society dedicates a significant portion of its tax revenues to welfare programs that fund health care, food assistance, housing aid, and other forms of giving to improve the lot of the poorest among us. These efforts are often inadequate and poorly designed. But their very existence reflects the fact that most members of society feel a genuine obligation to do something to reduce the extreme inequality that leaves so many millions without the resources necessary for a secure and fulfilling life.

Charity and welfare programs are well-intended efforts to lessen the damage done by the capitalist system. But a real solution requires a change in the system itself.

CAPITALIST MAN VERSUS REAL MAN

THE SYSTEMIC PROBLEM STARTS WITH the assumptions we make about human nature. Indifference to other human beings is deeply embedded in the current conceptual framework of economics. The neoclassical theory of economics is based on the belief that a human being is basically a personal-gain-seeking being. It assumes that maximizing personal profit is the core of economic rationality. This assumption encourages a form of behavior toward other human beings that deserves to be described by far harsher words than mere *"indifference"*—words like *greed, exploitation,* and *selfishness.* According to many economic thinkers, selfishness is not even a problem; it is, in fact, the highest virtue of Capitalist Man.

I for one would not like to live in a world where selfishness is the highest virtue. But the deeper problem with economic theory is that it is so sharply divorced from reality. Thankfully, in the real world, almost no one behaves with the absolute selfishness that is supposed to govern Capitalist Man.

And while we are discussing Capitalist Man, we may ask whether this expression is also supposed to refer to Capitalist Woman. Are they the same? Does Capitalist Man stand for Capitalist Woman? Or should we create a Real Person to represent both?

The Real Person is a composite of many qualities. He or she enjoys and cherishes relationships with other human beings. Real People are sometimes selfish, but just as often they are caring, trusting, and selfless. They work not only to make money for themselves but also to benefit others; to enhance society; to protect the environment; and to help bring more joy, beauty, and love into the world.

Plenty of evidence proves the existence of these altruistic drives. If they did not exist, no one would take on the difficult jobs that make our world a better place. The fact that millions of people around the world choose to be schoolteachers, social workers, nurses, and firefighters when other opportunities for making a comfortable living are available to them proves that selfishness is not a universal value. The fact that millions of other people work to help others in their communities as social activists, nonprofit workers, volunteers, counselors, and mentors offers further evidence.

Even in the world of business, where you might assume that Capitalist Man reigns supreme, the virtues of selflessness and trust play a vital role. A clear example is that of Grameen Bank in Bangladesh. The entire bank is built on trust. No collateral is requested, no legal documents are demanded, no proof of "creditworthiness" is required. Most of the borrowers are illiterate and have no assets; many have never even handled money before. They are women who once had no place in the financial system. The idea of lending money to them to start their own businesses was considered crazy by conventional bankers and economists.

In fact, the entire system of Grameen Bank was regarded as impossible.

Yet today, Grameen Bank lends out over US$2.5 billion a year to 9 million poor women on the basis of trust only. It enjoys a repayment rate (as of 2016) of 98.96 percent. And microcredit banks that run on the same principles are operating successfully in many other countries, including the United States. For example, Grameen America has nineteen branches in twelve US cities with 86,000 borrowers, all women, who receive business startup loans averaging around US$1,000. As of 2017, the loans disbursed by Grameen America total over US$600 million, and the repayment rate is over 99 percent.

If human beings truly fit the mold of Capitalist Man, the borrowers from these trust-based banks would simply default on their loans and keep the money. As a result, Grameen Bank would quickly cease to exist. Its long-term success demonstrates the fact that Real Man is a very different—and much better—creature than Capitalist Man.

Nonetheless, many economists, business leaders, and government experts continue to think and act as if Capitalist Man is real, and as if selfishness is the only motivation behind human behavior. As a result, they perpetuate economic, social, and political systems that encourage selfishness and make it more difficult for people to practice the selfless, trusting behaviors millions of them instinctively prefer.

Consider, for example, the measurement systems we have created to gauge economic growth. Gross domestic product (GDP) measures the monetary value of all the finished goods and services produced within a country's borders in a specific time period. GDP is carefully measured by government agencies and widely reported in the news media. It is often treated as a measurement of the success of a country's economic system. Governments have even fallen as a result of perceived shortfalls in GDP growth.

Yet human society is an integrated whole. It consists of much more than the economic activity measured by GDP. Its success or failure should be measured in a consolidated way, not purely on the basis of an aggregate of narrowly selected economic information about individual performance.

GDP does not and cannot tell the whole story. Activities that do not require money changing hands are not counted as part of GDP—which means that, in effect, many of the things real human beings cherish most are treated as having no value. By contrast, money spent on weapons of war and other activities that harm people's health or despoil the environment are counted as part of GDP, despite the fact that they produce suffering and contribute nothing to human happiness.

GDP may accurately measure the selfish behavior of Capitalist Man. But it does not capture the success of Real Man. We need some new form of measurement to do that. Perhaps we should explore ways to calculate a new measurement of GDP that "nets out" the harms done to human beings. This will be a GDP minus behaviors that harm human beings and prevent them from fulfilling their potential—poverty, unemployment, illiteracy, crime, violence, racism, oppression of women, and so on. Obviously there will be challenges in accurately defining and measuring this new "net GDP," but we shouldn't abandon the idea just because it is difficult. Why settle for a measurement that is easy to calculate but leads the world to an inaccurate assessment of its economic health?[5]

Misleading measurement systems are just one symptom of the problems caused by our flawed economic thinking. Another is our failure to channel technological and social changes so they benefit all people rather than a chosen few. The last half century has seen a dramatic expansion of global trade and economic integration, thanks to improvements in transportation, communication, and information technology, as well as the gradual reduction of political and social barriers. This new era of globalization should have led to the creation of a global human family enjoying greater closeness, harmony, and friendship than ever before. But in practice, globalization has also generated enormous tension and hostility. It is placing people and nations in a confrontational posture, each striving to enhance its own selfish interests. The zero-sum assumptions built into our economic theory encourage people to look for ways to become "winners" in the economic battle—which requires turning everyone else into "losers." One result has been an alarming rise in nationalism, xenophobia, mistrust, and fear.

So we live with a philosophical paradox. Many economic theorists, journalists and pundits, and political leaders continue to proclaim that free-market capitalism is a perfect mechanism that only needs to be fully unleashed to solve all of humanity's problems. Yet at the same time our society tacitly confesses the shortcomings of the free market and channels billions of dollars every year toward remedial efforts. Unfortunately, these efforts are largely ineffective—as the continued concentration of wealth in a few hands and its painful effects on all of us makes clear.

A new way of thinking is needed.

A Redesigned Economic Engine

Deep in our hearts, we all recognize that the old dreams of the economic theorists have been exposed as fairy tales. The existing capitalist engine is producing more damage than solutions. It needs to be redesigned, piece by piece—or replaced by an entirely new engine.

My experience with Grameen Bank has helped me to imagine what such a redesigned engine might look like. I launched the bank without having any ambitious goals; I simply wanted to make life a little better for poor women in the villages of my home country. But over the past decades

I have increasingly found myself engaged in redesigning the economic engine and trying out the new model in the real world. I've been very happy to see how effectively it addresses the problems created by the old engine.

The redesigned economic engine has three basic elements. First, we need to embrace the concept of social business—a new form of enterprise based on the human virtue of selflessness. Second, we need to replace the assumption that human beings are job seekers with the new assumption that human beings are entrepreneurs. Third, we need to redesign the entire financial system to make it work efficiently for the people at the bottom of the economic ladder.

Thousands of people in countries around the world have joined the effort to build a new version of capitalism. Hundreds of social businesses have been established around the world, in addition to the ones I have created in Bangladesh since Grameen Bank, to address the problems that traditional capitalism has created.

In the chapters that follow, I'll describe these experiences and the lessons they offer about the enormous potential of fresh economic thinking to transform human society. If we are willing to reconsider the assumptions underlying neoclassical economics, we can develop a new economic system designed to truly serve the needs of real human beings, creating a world in which everyone has the opportunity to fulfill his or her creative potential.

2

CREATING A NEW CIVILIZATION: THE COUNTERECONOMICS OF SOCIAL BUSINESS

W E'VE SEEN THAT THE PROBLEM of wealth concentration has continued to grow worse in recent years, even as awareness of the problem has expanded and deepened. Ordinary people in one country after another have risen up in anger against the unfairness of the current economic system. Some politicians have seized upon the issue to attract votes and, unfortunately, to stoke feelings of resentment and hostility against scapegoat groups like immigrants and minorities. Yet the trend toward greater wealth concentration has continued unchecked. Can it be stopped? Or is it an inevitable by-product of any free market system?

My firm answer is, yes, it can be done. There is no reason to blame the free market. The blame should go to something beyond that—to the way we have interpreted human nature in capitalist theory. There lies the root cause. We restrict the types of players who can play in the free market. Today we allow only selfishness-driven players into the market. If we allow selflessness-driven players into the market as well, the situation changes completely.

Old ways of addressing inequality, through charitable efforts and government programs, cannot solve the problem. People can solve it through actions that break away from the traditional capitalist mind-set. All they have to do is to express their willingness to participate in creating selflessness-driven businesses—that is, social businesses appropriate to their own capacity to solve human problems.

That simple action changes the whole world. If millions of people of every economic status take the lead in solving human problems, we can slow down and ultimately reverse the whole process of wealth concentration. This will encourage companies to bring their experience and technology to bear in creating powerful social business. Governments will create the right kind of policy packages to facilitate these initiatives from people and businesses. As a result, the momentum for change will become unstoppable.

The Paris Agreement—A Victory for the People

LET ME DRAW A COMPARISON to another dire global problem, one that is closely related to the problem of rising wealth concentration—the problem of climate change.

People around the world have been increasingly becoming aware of the dangers posed by human-driven climate change—just as they are aware of the problem of growing wealth concentration. Yet the trend toward worsening climate conditions has continued.

In recent years, our planet has experienced month after month marked by the hottest temperatures on record. Arctic

sea ice has reached record low levels; ocean levels continue
to rise; extreme weather conditions are becoming more common. All these changes have happened relatively quietly, without drawing the attention they deserve.

Many climate activists have been trying their best to attract
the focus of the people and the policy makers to this problem
through public demonstrations and communications through
the news media. So have the overwhelming majority of scientists who have studied the issue. They've been telling the world
that if we don't take heed of such troubling milestones, before
long we will reach the point of no return—a tipping point at
which "positive feedback" caused by natural systems will make
it almost impossible to reverse the dire, destructive trend.[1]
Common people, particularly young people, around the world
have been campaigning for years to make their governments
recognize this global peril and take actions to stop it.

Finally, in 2015, after forty years of effort, those actions
began to happen.

At the 2015 Paris Climate Conference, also known as
COP21, representatives from around the world agreed for the
first time on a practical framework to limit and reduce the
production of greenhouse gases that are driving global climate
change. Adopted by consensus on December 12, 2015, the
Paris Agreement has now been signed by 195 nations that are
members of the United Nations Framework Convention on
Climate Change (UNFCCC).

I was thrilled and inspired by the outcome of COP21. After forty years of battles between believers in climate change
and nonbelievers, the believers finally won. Dedicated scientists and activists persuaded people everywhere that the world
is in real danger and that we must act collectively to avert it.
As a result, nations big and small, rich and poor, signed on to

a legally binding agreement with the potential to protect our planet from impending climate disaster.

Political leaders from many countries played an important role in this victory. But more important, I see Paris as a victory of the people, led by the committed activists who never gave up campaigning for their cause.

Normally we look to governments to mobilize public opinion behind their decisions. In the case of global warming, it was the reverse. It was the citizens of the world who mobilized their governments. Thousands of activists fought an uphill battle to convince politicians, business leaders, and their fellow citizens that climate change was real and serious, yet also preventable. Millions who started on the sidelines gradually became activists themselves. They voted for political candidates who supported climate action. Political parties with green platforms began winning elections, both locally and nationally. Even during the Paris conference itself, hundreds of thousands of people marched at events in countries around the world, united in calling for a clean-energy future to save everything they love.[2] Actions like these helped put pressure on the politicians to set aside their differences and act in service to the common good.

The problem of climate change is far from solved. There are still powerful efforts of resistance launched by fossil-fuel companies and others who oppose change for purely selfish reasons. In the United States, the election of Donald Trump, who announced plans to withdraw the US from the Paris Agreement, shows that the battle against willful ignorance continues. But momentum finally appears to be on the right side.

COP21 made me hopeful that a citizens' movement can make the world ready to overcome another impending disaster. Climate change and wealth concentration both pose serious dangers to the future of human society. One poses a physical threat against the natural systems that make life on this planet livable; the other poses a social, political, and economic threat against the right of all people to live in dignity, freedom, and peace, pursuing goals that are higher than mere survival. These two problems have their inner links, too, as highlighted by the Trump election victory. Anger on the part of people who feel victimized by the economic system helped lead to Trump's election—which now threatens the future of the Paris Agreement.

If the collective efforts of citizens from all sections of society, led by a committed group of scientists and activists, can change public opinion about climate change and force action by political leaders, I believe that we can follow the same road map to galvanize the forces needed to protect humanity from the danger of ever-intensifying wealth concentration.

Extreme wealth concentration is not an unalterable fate that humankind was born with. Since it is our own creation, we can solve it through our own efforts. Our collective blocked mind prevents us from seeing the forces that are pushing us toward the inevitable social explosion. Our efforts should be directed toward unblocking our minds. We must challenge the existing paradigms that led the world into this problem.

Most attempts to reduce the problem of wealth concentration focus on income redistribution, taking from the top through progressive taxation and giving to the bottom through various transfer payment programs.

Unfortunately, it's almost impossible for a democratic government to achieve any significant success through a redistribution program. The wealthiest people from whom the government is supposed to collect heavy taxes are politically very powerful. They use their disproportionate influence to restrain the government from taking any meaningful step against their interest.

The real solution is to address the cause, not the effect. We need to redesign the economic framework of our society by moving from a system driven purely by personal interest to a system in which both personal and collective interests are recognized, promoted, and celebrated.

Grameen Bank: Rethinking the Financial System

The idea of redesigning our economic framework in order to build a more egalitarian society may sound impossible. But I know it is possible because I can see it happening.

My experience with the development of new economic framework begins with Grameen Bank. And Grameen Bank came into existence after circumstances pushed me into doing things that I knew nothing about. It is a story that I have told before, in my books *Banker to the Poor* (1999) and *Creating a World Without Poverty* (2007). But because you may not have read those books, and because the story is directly relevant to the message of economic reinvention I am presenting, let me now briefly summarize the story of how Grameen Bank came to be.

The terrible famine that struck Bangladesh in 1974 motivated me and many others to try to do something about the poverty that was causing so much suffering in the country. My efforts to grow irrigated crops in the village of Jobra near where I was teaching economics introduced me to the poor people who lived there and the impact on them of the money-lending operation in the village. I soon realized that the moneylenders who imposed extremely harsh conditions on borrowers were holding the poor villagers in a condition not far removed from slavery. To help the villagers, I started lending them money from my own pocket. This was the beginning of a journey that led to the creation of Grameen Bank.

Since I had no experience in or knowledge of banking, I had to look to the conventional banks to learn how they worked. But because their methods had failed to serve the poor people of Jobra, I couldn't simply imitate them. Instead, each time I learned how the conventional banks did things, I did the reverse. As a result, the institution I created turned out to be the antithesis of a conventional bank.

Conventional banks like to operate in the big cities where businesses and rich people locate their offices. Grameen Bank works exclusively in the villages of Bangladesh. (In fact, the name Grameen Bank simply means "Village Bank" in the Bangla language.)

Conventional banks are owned and managed by rich people. Grameen Bank is mostly owned by the poor women who are its customers; poor women make up its board and decide its policies.

Conventional banks, particularly in Bangladesh, serve mostly men. Grameen Bank focuses on women, empowering them to become entrepreneurs and to lift their families out of poverty.

Conventional banks believe that the poor are not creditworthy. Grameen Bank established for the first time in history the fact that poor people, especially poor women, are highly creditworthy and in fact can be trusted to repay their loans at a higher rate than most rich borrowers.

Conventional banks lend on the basis of collateral (property offered by a borrower to guarantee loan repayment) and strict legal agreements drafted by lawyers. Grameen Bank is both collateral-free and lawyer-free. We have developed a banking system based completely on trust.

The banking system developed by Grameen Bank, known as microfinance, has gradually spread to countries around the world, mainly through the work of nonprofit, nongovernmental organizations (NGOs). Microfinance has become so successful that, in recent years, major development organizations like the World Bank, the International Monetary Fund (IMF), and the United Nations have taken an interest in promoting more inclusive financial programs. They've come—grudgingly—to accept our contention that poor people can and should be included in the financial system.

Unfortunately, current efforts to increase the inclusiveness of the banking system consist mainly of programs that encourage conventional banks to provide limited, often high-cost financial services to the poor. The failure of these efforts shows that true inclusiveness in banking can't be achieved through today's conventional financial institutions. These financial institutions are built on principles and modes of operation that exclude almost half of the world's population.

Rich people's banks are not designed to serve the nonrich. They may make some token gestures in that direction under pressure from above, but these won't constitute even 1 percent of their business. The unbanked of the world need access to real banking, not a handful of tiny programs undertaken mainly as public relations ploys.

My work with microcredit led me to question the very basics of the banking system. I discovered that real human beings are much bigger than the human beings assumed in the classical economic theory on which today's banking system is based. Grameen Bank's microfinance idea flourished globally because NGOs took it up. But NGOs are not equipped with the appropriate legal powers for filling the economic vacuum left by existing financial institutions. An empty space is waiting for a set of specially designed financial institutions that can provide the unbanked with all types of financial services designed exclusively for them, rather than offering them microsized loans through conventional institutions, which do little to solve the underlying problem.

Existing financial institutions are the conduit through which wealth concentration occurs and gathers momentum. They will continue to make the problem of wealth concentration worse in the future. If we are serious about wanting to slow the trend of wealth concentration, we need to do two things about the financial system. First, we need to redesign the current banking system so that it ceases to act as the facilitating vehicle for wealth concentration. Second, we need to build a new set of financial institutions to deliver financial services to the poor. Grameen Bank—owned mostly by poor people and designed specifically to serve their needs and their interests—is a model for this new banking system.

My work with poor women through Grameen Bank turned out to be my first step in a journey of discovery that led to deeper insights about our entire economic system. Since the establishment of Grameen Bank, I have created many other initiatives designed to broaden the system and make it more accessible to all.

SOCIAL BUSINESS AND THE FIRST STEPS
TOWARD A NEW ECONOMIC FRAMEWORK

WORKING TO PROVIDE BANKING TO the poor led me to discover many other problems of the poor. I tried to address these problems one by one. I always tried to solve each problem by creating a new business. This approach made sense to me because businesses are naturally organized to achieve concrete goals—to provide goods or services that people need, want, and will pay for. People who launch businesses and those who work for them usually have a clear sense of what they are trying to accomplish. This was the spirit that I tried to incorporate in my efforts to address people's problems.

Over time, starting businesses became a habit with me. Every time I confronted a problem, I created a business to solve it. Soon I had created many companies and company-like independent projects, providing goods and services for poor people that included housing, sanitary facilities, affordable health care, renewable energy, improved nutrition, clean drinking water, nursing education, and many more.

When I started creating these businesses, I had no grand vision in mind. I was simply trying to address the most serious problems of the poor people I was serving. But over time, the businesses I launched gradually started displaying some common features. They were created as self-sustaining businesses, generating revenues through the sale of goods and services. I had to do it this way because otherwise the businesses would soon run out of money and cease being of use to anyone. However, although the businesses generated more money than they spent, I made sure that no one was allowed to take any personal profit out of them. After all, my goal was to help the poor, not to enrich business owners. So the investors who provided capital to launch the businesses were able to get back their initial investments, but nothing more. After the invested amount was paid back to the investor, any profit earned by the companies was plowed back into the companies for improvement and expansion, so that more poor people could benefit.

Eventually I realized that my experiments had led to the creation of a new type of business. I called it *social business*.

I defined a social business as "a nondividend company dedicated to solving human problems." It was a concept that arose not from theorizing or speculation but from my practical experience working with villagers to solve tough social problems in one of the poorest countries on Earth at that time.

I was amazed by the results. I found it surprisingly easy to solve a human problem by creating an organization designed as a business with the sole mission of providing a human benefit to those in need.

At first, I wondered why no one before me had come up with the concept of social business. Why had the world left the challenge of solving social problems to governments and charities alone? The answer lay in economic theory, which gave businesses one and only one mandate: to generate profits and individual wealth. I found that the same tool can be used for a completely different purpose—namely, to solve human problems. I found it extremely powerful in getting the job done. Suddenly all the creative power of business could be marshaled behind the cause of making the world a better place.

On a more fundamental level, the blind spot in economic theory can be traced to a blind spot in the assumptions it makes about human nature. A businessperson is supposed to be driven solely by self-interest. As the saying goes, "Business is business." Profit and profit alone is its purpose, and this is supposed to suffice to satisfy the wishes of any business owner.

But human beings are not moneymaking robots. They are multidimensional beings with both selfishness and selflessness. When I create a social business, I am allowing the selfless side of my personality to be expressed through business. Traditional economic thinking considers this impossible; it says that selflessness cannot be part of the business world and is only to be expressed in the world of charity. But why? Why shouldn't the business world be an unbiased playground offering scope for both selfishness and selflessness? Why shouldn't economics textbooks introduce two types of businesses to students—traditional self-interest-driven businesses and selflessness-driven social businesses? Let the young people themselves decide which they would prefer to pursue—or perhaps a bit of both, at different times in their lives or even at the same time.

In the decades since I began talking about social business, the concept has gone from being an obscure idea exemplified by just a handful of companies in Bangladesh into a worldwide movement, with advocates and practitioners in many countries all over the planet. Universities are opening social business centers where the idea is being studied, developed, and taught. Multinational corporations are coming forward to set up social businesses as independent companies. Thousands of young people are getting attracted to the idea and are launching entrepreneurial social business ventures to tackle social problems in their own communities.

To encourage these developments, my colleagues in the social business movement and I have created funds that provide seed money to help would-be entrepreneurs turn their dreams into realities. When young people come up with smart social business ideas, we invest in their companies, provide expert coaching and guidance, and help them achieve financial independence. Once they are successful, they buy back our investment shares without giving the investors any profit. The money is then freed up to help launch another social business, and then another and another.

We have also been creating social business funds to finance unemployed young people to become personal-profit-making entrepreneurs—job creators rather than job seekers. Existing conventional banks and financial institutions aren't designed to fill this need; they have no interest in getting involved with unemployed young people who have no collateral and no credit history. That's why special funds are needed for this purpose. Now many young people are coming forward to set up their conventional businesses in partnership with our funds. Out of this partnership, the social business funds get back their investment money, with no interest and no profit, plus a fixed transfer fee to cover their costs of administration. We've found that social business funds that finance entrepreneurship can be a powerful tool for lifting individuals, families, and entire communities out of poverty.

To participate in the Nobin Udyokta (New Entrepreneurs) program that we created in Bangladesh—most often referred to, simply, as the Nobin program—all that a young person must do is come up with a business idea. Once the business plan is approved, the person gets the money to set up his or her personal-profit-making company. Participants don't have to create a social business (although they can if they wish). From our side, we create our social business entrepreneurship funds as social businesses. They are financially self-sustaining and their profit does not get passed on to any owner or investor, except for paying back the original investment they made.

Now our social business funds are approving an average of one thousand business proposals per month. Imagine—a thousand unemployed rural youth becoming entrepreneurs every month! And during 2017, we expect the numbers to roughly double, to almost two thousand per month.

I'll explain more about the workings of the New Entrepreneurs program later in this book. For now, let me emphasize that its success is a natural outgrowth of one of the most

important discoveries we made through running Grameen
Bank—the discovery that everybody has built-in capacity to
be an entrepreneur.

The DNA of entrepreneurship is common to all human
beings. We began life on this planet as independent hunters
and gatherers, seeking our own livelihood from the resources
provided so abundantly in the world around us. The ability
to find a way to support oneself remains latent, even today, in
every individual.

Supporting entrepreneurship is the basic way of overcoming one of the fatal flaws in the mainstream economic
model—the forced dependence on jobs, government or corporate, and the assumption that, as job creators, governments
and corporations are the only drivers of economic growth. I
see no reason why young people in the developed world cannot become entrepreneurs in the same way as young people
in Bangladesh. The key is to create financing institutions that
will support their startups in an accessible, friendly way.

The Countereconomics of Entrepreneurship

Looking at the growth and spread of social business so
far, we can see the emergence of an alternative to the traditional, incomplete system of economics that has dominated
the worldview of most people in recent history. Once we replace two basic assumptions of mainstream economic thinking with the new realities revealed by social business, a new,
more complete, accurate, and effective countereconomics
emerges.

First, we need to replace the assumption that people are
by nature selfish—and that, therefore, selfishness is the core

driving force behind all economic progress—with the new assumption that people are both selfish and selfless, and that
both motivations can be applied to economic activity.

Second, we need to replace the assumption that nearly all
people are born to spend their lives working for other people
with the new assumption that all people are born entrepreneurs, packed with unlimited creative capabilities.

Once these shifts in thinking are made, we can appreciate
the power of new economic thinking in addressing the problems created by the existing economic framework. We can
employ social business to tackle ancient maladies like poverty,
hunger, disease, environmental degradation, and many more.
In addition, we can also create opportunities for millions of
unemployed young people to put their wasted talents to appropriate use by treating them as entrepreneurs.

Social business is about using creativity to solve human
problems in a sustainable way. Just as microfinance started
out in Bangladesh and led the way for the world to get used
to the idea of trust-based banking, our New Entrepreneurs
program for unemployed youth will also pave a new path for
positive change in the rest of the world.

No matter where they live, young unemployed people are
primarily looking for a basic income to support themselves.
But they also have a suppressed hunger for finding meaning in
their lives. Fortunately, the current generation of young people is in a unique position to succeed in the quest for meaning
once they feel relieved from the search for a basic livelihood.
They are a generation that was born with amazing technologies in their hands. Thanks to the incredible economics of
high technology, even young people in the rural villages of
Asia, Africa, and South America can get access to the unprecedented computing power of smart phones and other mobile

devices. This has made them potentially the most powerful generation in human history. They grew up knowing that touch screens, remote controls, and mobile apps can empower them to do anything they want. They may not realize the full dimensions of the power that they possess, but they sense that they have the potential to make all impossibles possible.

Today's rising generation—hundreds of millions of young people in cities, towns, suburbs, and villages around the world, from Bangladesh to Brazil, Albania to Haiti, India to Ireland, Japan to the United States—has the talent, energy, intelligence, idealism, and generosity to transform the world. These young people are capable of creating a new civilization that has escaped from the shadows of poverty, unemployment, and environmental degradation. Now we need to create the new economic system that will unlock their powers and allow them to realize their potential. In the remaining chapters of this book, I'll explain what this new economic system could look like, and I'll describe some of the hopeful signs that this system is already beginning to take shape.

THE THREE ZEROS

3

ZERO POVERTY:
BRINGING AN END TO
INCOME INEQUALITY

WHAT COMES TO MIND WHEN you think about the word *entrepreneurship*? Maybe you think about California's Silicon Valley, with its countless high-tech manufacturers, app developers, and software companies. Or maybe you think of one of today's fast-growing hubs for biotechnology, robotics, and computers, such as Boston, Massachusetts; Sydney, Australia; Bangalore, India; or Vancouver, Canada.

You probably *don't* think about the West African nation of Uganda. Yet in a 2015 report, the organization Global Entrepreneurship Monitor (GEM) ranked Uganda as the most entrepreneurial nation in the world.[1] According to GEM, more than 28 percent of the population of Uganda has started a business in the last three and a half years—more than six times the percentage (4.3 percent) in the United States. Other studies estimate that more than 80 percent of Ugandans will start a business sometime during their lives.

If you find this surprising, it may be because your image of an entrepreneur is too limited. You don't need a degree in engineering or computer science to launch a business. Many entrepreneurs take the leap by opening a small shop, buying a goat or cow, starting a taxi service with a single vehicle, or offering a few handmade craft items for sale. Just like the high-flying entrepreneurs of Silicon Valley, they are investing their time and resources in a business based on a creative idea that they believe in. Over time, if they are successful, they may expand their operations, creating jobs, generating wealth, and helping to grow their local economies.

That's exactly what millions of mostly small entrepreneurial businesses are doing all over Uganda, just as in many developing countries. In the process, they are helping to gradually lift their country and its people out of poverty. They demonstrate one of the fundamental principles of the new economic structure I advocate—that the skills and instincts that make entrepreneurship possible are shared by all human beings, not just a select few. And Uganda is not alone. In emerging countries all over the world, you'll find the same burst of entrepreneurship at the bottom of the economy. But unfortunately, no support system to match the need exists in any country—including in Uganda, where the existing system has hampered the development of a culture of economic freedom, despite the strong entrepreneurial instincts of so many of the country's citizens.

Uganda is one of seven countries of the world in which Yunus Social Business (YSB) now operates. YSB is a nonprofit organization dedicated to spreading the concept of social business, training and supporting pioneers who are interested in launching social businesses, and working with corporations and business leaders who want to create companies or divisions dedicated to social business. By helping to grow the new economy sector in the countries where it operates, YSB is promoting the emergence of self-sustaining companies that are forging solutions to problems like poverty, unemployment, and environmental degradation. Thus, it is helping to create the new economic structure we badly need to supplement the incomplete structure of traditional capitalism.

For a simple but powerful example of how it works, consider one of the social businesses that YSB has helped to develop—a company called Golden Bees, headquartered in Kampala, the capital city of Uganda.

Agriculture, both for local consumption and for export, is the leading industry of Uganda, representing the largest share of GDP of any economic sector. But small farmers in local villages have difficulty getting access to national and international markets with the goods they produce. This limits the income they can earn and makes it harder for them to lift their families and communities above the subsistence level.

One of the most promising growth sectors for these farmers is beekeeping. The bees, of course, produce honey, which is a popular commercial product in Africa, used as a sweetener in many kinds of foods and as a staple in the kitchens of countless families. Bees also produce a large and growing array of other products, some of them even more profitable than honey. These include beeswax, an important ingredient in many kinds of cosmetics and health care products; bee venom, harvested from the stingers of the bees, which is popular for medicinal purposes; and propolis, sometimes called "bee glue," a resinous substance being studied by modern researchers for its potential medical uses.

Golden Bees is a social business whose mission is to bring beekeeping within reach of thousands of small Ugandan farmers. It does this by selling essential beekeeping goods and services to the farmers, training them in beekeeping techniques, and then collecting, processing, and marketing the products they create. The income Golden Bees generates through its activities keeps the business afloat; any profits are reinvested in expansion, so that the services can be made available to even larger numbers of farmers.

As of mid-2016, Golden Bees has built a network of over 1,200 farmers, with hundreds more waiting to receive training and equipment from the company. The smallest participant maintains just three beehives, while the largest has an array of five hundred. The company operates three small shops located in farming regions near the capital city, where they sell honey and bee products (thereby generating revenues that help to pay worker salaries); provide training and consulting support to local beekeepers; and sell beehive boxes, beekeeper's suits to protect farmers from stings when harvesting honey, and other equipment. The shops also provide centralized collection sites for honey and other products, making it easier for farmers to deliver their wares to Golden Bees for processing.

A chain of about eighty supermarkets in Kampala sells the honey and other products produced by Golden Bees. Even more promising, the company is expanding its reach into national and international markets. Orders for beeswax have begun to arrive from companies in China, Japan, and Denmark, and pharmaceutical labs around the world are looking for supplies of Ugandan propolis. To supply these markets, Golden Bees is working on refining its products so they'll meet the stringent quality standards set by the international manufacturers—another task that would be impossible for one or a few small farmers to manage.

The story of Golden Bees is an example of the power of entrepreneurship to help poor people—and even entire communities—escape from poverty, as well as providing much-needed extra income for families that are already above the poverty line. The farmers of Uganda have always had the determination, intelligence, and work ethic needed to launch and maintain profitable beekeeping businesses on a scale appropriate to their own resources. But they lacked the tools and information to get started, as well as the business structure needed to connect them to the national and international markets. Golden Bees provides them with what they've lacked—and lets them do the rest. It shows how new forms of business can help to unlock the power of entrepreneurship, allowing poor people to lift themselves and their communities out of poverty through their own creative efforts.

Three Big Failures of Our Economic System

For too long, we've tolerated the persistence of poverty, unemployment, and environmental destruction, as if these are natural calamities completely out of human control, or, at best, unavoidable costs of economic growth. They are not. They are failures of our economic system—and since the economic system was created by human beings, these failures can be corrected if human beings choose to replace that economic system with a new system that more accurately reflects human nature, human needs, and human desires.

Remember, the central problem with capitalism as it is now practiced is that the system recognizes only one goal—the selfish pursuit of individual profit. As a result, only businesses designed around this goal are recognized and supported. Yet millions of people around the world are eager to pursue other goals, including the elimination of poverty, unemployment, and environmental degradation. All three can be dramatically reduced if we simply begin designing businesses with these goals in mind. And that is where social business plays a crucial role.

Social business offers advantages that are available neither to profit-maximizing companies nor to traditional charities. The freedom from profit pressures and from the demands of profit-seeking investors helps make social businesses viable even in circumstances where current capitalist markets fail—where the rate of return on an investment is near zero, but where the social return is very high. And because a social business is designed to generate revenues and thereby become self-sustaining, it is free from the need to constantly attract new streams of donor funding to stay afloat, which drains the time and energy of so many people in the nonprofit arena.

Thus, the economics of social business can be simple and sustainable, as illustrated by successful experiments that have already been launched in both the developing world and the wealthy nations.

We live in a particularly suitable time for these experiments with new forms of business, since electronic technologies for information and communication can play a huge role in amplifying the power of individual entrepreneurs. A social business owner who devises a product or service that helps the poor or benefits society in some other way may be able to attract a wide market by using social networking and other online tools to spread the word. Thanks to the Internet, good ideas can spread more rapidly, and proven business models can grow to scale more quickly and easily than ever. Health care, education, marketing, financial services, and many other economic arenas can be revolutionized through the combined power of social business and technology.

It's exciting to observe how these new economic concepts have been spreading around the globe through the efforts of entrepreneurs, executives, academics, students, and political leaders. Now it's time to apply the potential of social business to solving the problems of inequality, unemployment, and environmental decay—all symptoms of the broken engine of capitalism.

We owe it to future generations to begin moving toward a world of three zeros: zero poverty, zero unemployment, and zero net carbon emissions. A new economic system in which social business plays an essential role can enable us to achieve this goal.

Rude Awakening: How Crises of Capitalism Have Exacerbated the Problem of Poverty

Humankind as a whole is living in a time of unparalleled prosperity, fueled in part by revolutions in knowledge, science, and technology, particularly information technology. This prosperity has changed the lives of many. Yet billions of people still suffer from poverty, hunger, and disease. And in the last decade, several major crises have combined forces to bring even greater misery and frustration to the world's bottom 4 billion people.[2]

Few people foresaw these crises. The twenty-first century began with high hopes and idealistic dreams, encapsulated in the UN initiative known as the Millennium Development Goals (MDGs). Many of us were convinced that the coming decades would bring unprecedented wealth and prosperity, not just for a few but for all people on this planet.

As I'll discuss later in this book, establishment of the MDGs led to significant progress on several fronts in the battle against poverty. Sadly, however, 2008 will go down in history as the year of a rude awakening about the gross weaknesses in our capitalist system. It was the year of the food price crisis, the oil price crisis, the financial crisis, and the ever-worsening environmental crisis. In combination, these crises caused a profound loss of faith among people who thought they had full understanding of and control over the global system. They also prevented the fulfillment of the hopeful promise represented by the MDGs.

Let's start by considering the food crisis. Early in 2008, the United Nations World Food Programme (WFP) reported dreadful news: more than 73 million people in seventy-eight countries were facing the reality of reduced food rations. We saw headlines reporting news of a sort that many people assumed we would never experience again: skyrocketing prices for staple foodstuffs like grains and vegetables (wheat alone having risen in price by 200 percent since the year 2000), food shortages in many countries, rising rates of death from malnutrition, and even food riots threatening the stability of countries around the globe.

Since the June 2008 peak in global food prices, prices have continued to fluctuate, reaching another record high in 2011. As of 2016, they had fallen slightly, bringing a bit of short-term relief to millions. But continuing high food prices have created tremendous pressure in the lives of poor people, for whom basic food can consume as much as two thirds of their income.[3]

Emergency programs to alleviate the worst results of the food crisis have been helpful. But while short-term relief efforts are essential to stave off the immediate effects of food shortages and prevent widespread famine, it's also important to step back and take a look at the broader causes of the crisis. We need to consider how the evolution of the world economy and, in particular, of the system whereby food is produced and distributed has led us to today's dilemma. Perhaps surprisingly, the economic, political, and business practices of the developed world have a profound impact on the availability of food in the poor nations of the world. Thus, solving the global food problem will require a redesign of the international framework, not merely a series of local or even regional reforms.

The current challenges have their roots in history. The Green Revolution of the 1950s and 1960s increased crop yields in Asia and Latin America and made many countries that had been reliant on food imports self-sufficient. Rates of hunger and malnutrition dropped significantly. The high-yield grain production made possible by the Green Revolution has been credited with saving the lives of up to a billion people.

Now, however, a series of interrelated trends has partially reversed the gains that the Green Revolution produced. Part of the problem has been the way in which globalization of food markets has been managed over the past three decades. I am a strong proponent of free trade; I believe that encouraging people and nations to exchange goods and services with one another will, in the long run, lead to greater prosperity for all. But like all markets, global markets need reasonable rules that will allow all participants an opportunity to benefit.

Today's global markets, unfortunately, are only partly free, and some of the restrictions and distortions that have been left in place have had devastating consequences for poor nations. The imbalances caused by this semi-free trade are distorting markets, raising prices, and even destroying agriculture in poor countries that once boasted enormous food surpluses.[4]

Subsidies for ethanol in countries like the United States are one example of this problem. Intended to encourage the growth of corn and soy to partially replace fossil fuels in gasoline, these subsidies may have made sense when oil cost US$20 a barrel. They were designed to make it economically viable to use biofuels as a partial substitute for relatively cheap and abundant oil. And they worked as intended, as shown by the fact that, in 2007, fully one quarter of the maize (corn) crop in the United States was used to manufacture ethanol.

However, these same subsidies cannot be justified when oil costs over US$50 a barrel (as it did in early 2017)—nor can the continuing subsidies for oil production enjoyed by large, highly profitable firms like ExxonMobil. Both sets of subsidies distort markets; lead to unintended ecological, social, and economic consequences; and should be phased out as quickly as possible. Otherwise, they will continue to drive up the price of basic foodstuffs both directly and indirectly, including by diverting farmland and other agricultural resources to the production of fuel rather than food.

Increased demand for meat has also distorted food price structures and contributed to worldwide food shortages. Growing prosperity in some of the world's poorest nations is, of course, a wonderful thing. Over the past three decades, millions of people have been able to lift themselves out of poverty. The credit goes to increased access to free markets, technological developments, and programs such as microcredit that make capital for investments available to those who were once shut out of the capitalist system.

But prosperity is bringing its own challenges. The amount of meat eaten by the typical Chinese citizen has increased from 20 kilograms per year in 1958 to over 50 kilograms today (still slightly lower than the US average of around 57 kilograms).[5] Similar increases have been seen in other large countries such as Indonesia and Bangladesh. Not only can more and more

people in these countries now afford meat, but they are shift-
ing to meat (and away from more traditional, low-meat diets)
as part of their adoption of a "modern" lifestyle.

Unfortunately, meat-eating is a relatively inefficient use
of natural resources. The number of nutritious calories delivered by meat is far lower than the calories humans can enjoy through direct intake of grains. Yet today, more and more
grain and other foodstuffs are being used to feed cattle rather
than human beings. By some measures, up to a third of the
world's grain production, as well as a third of the global fish
catch, is being used to feed livestock. And more and more of
the planet's farmlands are being diverted from the production
of food for human consumption and toward the growing of
grains for cattle feed.

These changes add several costly steps to the process by
which human life will ultimately be sustained. As a result
of dysfunctional agricultural choices such as the decision to
shift land use toward ethanol and meat production, even basic
foods are becoming more expensive.

Still other factors have worsened the food crisis for developing nations. One of these is the growing difficulty for farmers in poor nations to compete in the increasingly global food
markets. In effect, small farmers in developing nations are suffering because of the necessity to compete against large-scale
producers in the developed nations. It's a one-sided battle
that, so far, has led to devastating results for the poor farmers
of the world.

Increasing corporate control of agricultural resources is
also harming farmers in the developing world. As large agri-
businesses take near-monopoly control over seed stocks as well
as control over supplies of costly synthetic fertilizers and pes-
ticides, more and more small farms are driven out of business,

unable to afford the supplies they need to compete in the new global food market.

The cost of oil is a significant factor here, too. For example, many fertilizers are petroleum-based, which means that every increase in the cost of a barrel of oil drives up the cost of fertilizer. Of course, higher oil prices also drive up the cost of any activity that requires energy, including irrigation, running farm equipment, delivering goods to market, and shipping foods to and from processing plants.

All of these economic and social problems are growing worse just as global environmental trends are threatening the future of agriculture around the world. Climate change and drought are turning vast areas that were once fertile farm-lands into deserts. The need for new farmland and continuing urban sprawl are driving deforestation, which further acceler-ates global warming. Scientific simulations suggest that while climate change will slightly increase the total amount of land available for farming, the overall quality of croplands will decline. What's more, the regions most vulnerable to loss of farmland are already some of the most economically troubled areas of the world, including sub-Saharan Africa, the Middle East, and North Africa.[6]

One of the countries that is most immediately impacted is my homeland of Bangladesh, the world's most densely pop-ulated country, which is a flat country with 20 percent of its land less than 1 meter above sea level. As the sea level keeps rising, flooding in Bangladesh grows steadily worse and more destructive. It is an emerging case of environmental disaster leading immediately to human disaster.

Back in 2008, on top of the food crisis, the oil price cri-sis, and the environmental crisis, came the biggest crisis of all—the crushing collapse of the US financial system. Giant financial institutions along with major manufacturing firms like the automakers either went bankrupt or were kept alive through unprecedented government bailout packages.

Many reasons have been suggested for this historic economic collapse: excessive greed in the market place, the transformation of investment markets into gambling casinos, the failure of regulatory institutions, and so on. But one thing is clear: the financial system broke down because of a fundamental distortion of its basic purpose.

Credit markets were originally created to serve human needs—to provide businesspeople with capital to start or expand companies. In return for these services, bankers and other lenders earned a reasonable profit. Everyone benefited. In the twenty-first century, however, the credit markets were distorted by a relative handful of individuals and companies with a different goal in mind—to earn unrealistically high rates of return through clever feats of financial engineering. They repackaged mortgages and other loans into sophisticated instruments whose risk level and other characteristics were hidden or disguised. Then they sold and resold these instruments, earning a slice of profit on every transaction. All the while, investors eagerly bid up the prices, scrambling for unsustainable growth and gambling that the underlying weakness of the system would never come to light.

In time, the inevitable happened. The house of cards came tumbling down. And because of globalization, this financial tsunami spread all over the world.

In the end, the rich were not the worst sufferers from this financial crisis. Instead, most of the pain fell on the bottom 4 billion people on this planet, despite the fact that they were not responsible in any way for creating the crisis. While the rich continued to enjoy a privileged lifestyle, the bottom 4 billion people faced job and income losses that, for many, made the difference between life and death.

The combined effects of the financial crisis, the food crisis, the energy crisis, and the environmental crisis have continued to unfold in recent months and years, affecting the bottom 4 billion with special force. And while governments around the world responded to the crises by putting into place many emergency programs, including expensive bailout programs to prop up troubled financial institutions and giant corporations, they have not done enough to address the long-term problem of poverty. By focusing on support for giant institutions that are "too big to fail," they implied that billions of poor people are "too small to matter."

A new approach to capitalism that includes making space for social business offers hope to alleviate this problem.

Social Business as a Remedy for the Many Impacts of Poverty

The concept of social business crystallized in my mind through my experience with the Grameen companies. As I've explained, the idea emerged not as a theoretical concept but as a simple, practical tool for alleviating the worst effects of poverty in Bangladesh.

It's important to start with the realization that poverty is not created by poor people. It is created by an economic system in which all the resources tend to keep surging up toward the top, creating an ever-expanding mushroom head of wealth belonging to only one percent of the people. The image of a mushroom head describes the situation very well. The giant mushroom head represents the wealth ownership of the few, while the very long, thin stem hanging from it represents the wealth owned by the remaining 99 percent of the population. Over time, this stem gets thinner and longer, while the mushroom head gets bigger.

The word *inequality* is totally inadequate to describe this unsustainable and unacceptable situation. If you wanted to describe the difference between ants and elephants, you would certainly not use the word *inequality*!

We have to accept the fact that there is no semblance of "wealth distribution" in the current system. Instead, the system is built for one-way concentration, the way a raging forest fire sucks up all the oxygen in the forest. There is nothing in the system that can stop this process. It is designed for wealth monopoly rather than wealth distribution.

Within the current system, poor people are like bonsai trees. These trees start from the same seeds as the full-sized pines or birch trees found in nature. But because they are kept in tiny planters and have access to small amounts of water and other nutrients, bonsai trees never grow to their destined height. Instead, they grow to be tiny replicas of the full-sized trees.

It's the same with poor people. They are bonsai people. They remain stunted, like the bonsai trees. There is nothing wrong with the seeds from which the poor people grow. But the system does not allow them the same opportunities that are given to the nonpoor. As a result, they cannot use their creativity and entrepreneurship to grow as others do.

The new economic system we need is one that gives the bonsai people of the world the resources they need to grow straight, tall, and beautiful.

One of the most insidious and destructive characteristics of poverty is the way it attacks human happiness and

well-being in multiple dimensions. Each of these attacks re-
inforces and strengthens the others. For example, poor people are usually unable to get access to decent health care. As
a result, they experience more prolonged and serious bouts
of illness. Not only does this shorten their lives, but it also
makes it much harder for them to attend school or to work for
a living—which, in turn, drives them deeper into poverty. In
the same way, lack of clean drinking water, substandard housing, and little or no access to mobility all combine to condemn poor people to lives of struggle and misery, multiplying
the impacts of poverty and making it even harder for them to
escape.

Over the years, following the establishment of Grameen
Bank, I set up many financially sustainable projects and enterprises to address the problems of the poor. They included
enterprises for vegetable seed marketing to combat the widespread problem of night blindness among the children of poor
families and enterprises for sanitation and for safe drinking
water through hand tube wells. Later, I started launching formal companies to address many of the interlocking problems
faced by the poor in Bangladesh. Whether it was a company
to provide renewable energy, several companies to provide
health care, or a company to provide information technology
to the poor, we were always motivated by the desire to address
the social needs of those living in poverty.

We designed these businesses as income-generating companies, but only to ensure their sustainability so that the
products or services they provided could reach more and more
of the poor—and on an ongoing basis. In all these cases, the
social need was the only consideration; earning profit for individual owners or investors was no consideration at all. That
is how I realized that businesses could be built that way, from

the ground up, around specific social needs, without any motive of personal gain.

The concept of social business got international attention in 2006 when Grameen Bank launched a joint venture with Danone, the multinational food products company from France. (The story is told much more fully in my 2007 book *Creating a World Without Poverty*.) Grameen teamed up with Danone's chairman and then-CEO, Franck Riboud, to create a company that brings yogurt fortified with vitamins, minerals, and other essential nutrients to the undernourished children of rural Bangladesh. We sell the yogurt to poor families at an affordable price, charging just enough to make the company self-sustaining. (A cup of yogurt currently costs 10 Bangladeshi *taka,* the equivalent of 12 cents in US currency.) Beyond the return of Danone's and Grameen's original investment capital—the equivalent of about a million euros—neither Grameen nor Danone makes any money from this venture, according to the terms of our formal written agreement. We have one yogurt plant already operating in the vicinity of Bogra, a city north of the capital in Dhaka, and in time we hope to have more such plants throughout the country.

Grameen Danone Foods helps to alleviate the impact of poverty in several mutually reinforcing ways. Most obviously, the yogurt it sells brings health benefits to children who would otherwise suffer from diseases associated with malnutrition, as verified by a 2013 study conducted by a team of scientists with support from the Global Alliance for Improved Nutrition (GAIN).[7] And the presence of the yogurt factory in Bogra has brought other benefits to the community. The milk used in production is supplied by local farmers, giving them an additional source of regular income. Local women sell the yogurt commissions they earn. And local people trained by Danone run the factory itself as well as its distribution and marketing channels, bringing further vitality to the rural economy.

Grameen Danone Foods is just the first joint venture social business we launched. Now more and more companies are coming forward to partner with us to set up new social businesses. For example, we have created a joint venture with Veolia, a major water treatment and delivery company based in France, to deliver safe drinking water in the villages of Bangladesh. This joint venture operates a water treatment plant that brings clean water to fifty thousand villagers in an area of Bangladesh where the existing water supply is highly contaminated by arsenic. We sell the water to villagers at a price of just 3 cents per 10 liters. This makes the company sustainable, but no financial gain comes to Grameen or Veolia.

We have created other joint venture social businesses in Bangladesh with corporations that include Intel Corporation, BASF, Uniqlo, SK Dream, and Euglena.

Each of these businesses has its own unique story. Grameen Euglena, for example, traces its origin to a 1998 visit to Bangladesh by an eighteen-year-old student named Mitsuru Izumo. After an internship at Grameen Bank, Izumo became committed to addressing the problem of malnutrition. He switched his field of study from literature to agriculture and became intrigued by the remarkable properties of euglena, a single-celled organism that contains most of the elements needed for human survival. Believing that euglena could be developed as a super food for the world, Izumo focused on researching ways to produce it commercially. To market the product, he created his company, Euglena, in 2005, and it is now listed on the Tokyo stock exchange. In 2014, he launched Grameen Euglena as a co-venture with the Grameen Krishi Foundation. This social business produces euglena cookies for schoolchildren as well as mung beans, a nutritious legume, thereby boosting the incomes of some eight thousand farmers in Bangladesh.

Other social businesses in Bangladesh have been launched by Grameen independently rather than in partnership with an outside company. One of the problems we've sought to address is that of cataract blindness. This is another affliction that makes the lives of the poor miserable, although it is relatively easy to remedy through a routine operation.

To tackle this problem, in 2008, we opened a hospital in Bogra that provides eye exams and cataract surgery, financed on socially equitable principles. Fees provided by middle-class and well-off clients help to subsidize the care of those with little or nothing to contribute. All patients, of course, receive the same high quality of care, no matter how much or how little they pay. Within four years, the hospital became financially self-sustaining. A second hospital operating in the same fashion was opened in Barisal in southern Bangladesh in 2009; it achieved operational sustainability within three years. A third hospital was opened in the far north of Bangladesh in 2016, and as of 2017 a fourth is under construction. To date, our hospitals have treated over 1 million patients and performed more than fifty-five thousand vision-saving operations.

Another successful social business is Grameen Distribution, a rural marketing network we created in 2009 to sell useful, affordable commercial products at the doorstep of rural households. The poor women employed as members of the Grameen Marketing Network sell products that include mobile telephone handsets and accessories, solar panels and mini solar energy systems, chemically treated mosquito nets to reduce the incidence of malaria and other infectious diseases, and energy-efficient light fixtures and bulbs. With a market reach of over 1.5 million rural households, Grameen Distribution generates grassroots employment for many thousands of village women, increasing their family incomes by an average of US$37 per month. In a country where (for example) the minimum monthly wage in the huge garment industry is as low as US$68, that's a significant boost to a family's efforts to work their way out of poverty.[8]

One more social business example out of the many others I could name is the Grameen Caledonian College of Nursing, which opened its doors to students in March 2010. Nurses play a crucial role in the delivery of high-quality modern health care. But like most other poor countries, Bangladesh suffers a drastic shortage of professional nurses. Our population of 165 million is served by just twenty-three thousand nurses—over six thousand people per nurse. (By contrast, the 60 million citizens of the United Kingdom are served by 680,000 nurses, a ratio of eighty-eight people per nurse.) In part because of this shortage, some 87 percent of mothers in Bangladesh give birth without receiving professional medical support—another example of the mutually reinforcing impacts of poverty on the lives of the poor.

To tackle this problem, Grameen Healthcare Trust entered an agreement with Glasgow Caledonian University to launch a world-class college for the education of nurses and midwives in the capital city of Dhaka. Within months, an up-to-date curriculum was developed; academic and administrative staff were recruited; and modern training facilities, library, and labs were outfitted, along with living quarters for the students. The program started its journey in 2010 by admitting 40 students, all daughters of Grameen Bank borrowers. As of spring 2017, 634 students have been admitted to the college, and 223 have graduated with nursing diplomas. All of the graduates have received immediate positions in some of the country's leading hospitals. Another 81 students will complete their educations in 2017.

Furthermore, the college of nursing is already nearly self-sustaining operationally. Professor Barbara Parfitt, the college's founding principal, says that the school has deliberately resisted pressure to "follow the dollar" in its management practices. They design programs and policies to provide the highest-quality education and then find ways to cover the costs that make solid economic sense. That, in a nutshell, is the philosophy underlying social business.

All of these social businesses in Bangladesh—from my vegetable seed marketing project through the many others we've launched in the years since then—have helped to alleviate the worst effects of poverty in the villages of my country. As a result, millions of "bonsai families" have been able to access resources that are helping them achieve more and live richer, happier lives—resources ranging from clean drinking water to modern medical care to the skills and training needed to take on professional careers.

From Bangladesh to the World:
How the Spirit of Economic Experimentation
Is Now Spreading Globally

THE MORE DEEPLY I BECAME engaged in the lives of the poor, the more I recognized the importance of addressing the many problems faced by the poor—and the more I discovered that creatively designed social businesses, totally freed from the objective of personal profit, can be a forceful way to tackle those problems. The more I did, the more I liked them. The successes that social businesses have achieved in Bangladesh raised an obvious question: Could the same model be applied successfully in the rest of the world?

I am often invited to speak at university campuses and business conferences around the world. I take this opportunity to share my experiences and get feedback from the participants. In 2010, one of the universities where I spoke was the London School of Economics and Political Science (LSE). I did not know until some months later that a graduate of LSE among the students listening to my lecture would become immensely interested in the concept of social business.

This young woman, Saskia Bruysten, later attended another lecture that I gave in Berlin at an event titled the Vision Conference. This time, she came over after the lecture to talk to me. She asked me whether there was any opportunity for her and her friend Sophie Eisenmann to get involved in social businesses in Bangladesh and in other countries. To make it easy, I introduced her to Hans Reitz, a young entrepreneur from Wiesbaden, Germany. Hans had already been inspired by the social business idea and taken it upon himself to create social businesses in Germany and to promote the concept globally. In 2006, Hans founded an organization called Grameen Creative Lab (GCL) in Wiesbaden to pursue this goal.

Hans immediately invited Bruysten and her friend to join GCL. Bruysten was a management consultant working for Boston Consulting Group (BCG); she had an MBA degree and experience in both the business and nonprofit sectors. She and Eisenmann, her longtime school friend and roommate with a similar academic and professional background, left their jobs with BCG and joined GCL to dedicate themselves to the cause of promoting social business.

They worked with GCL for a year, then left to set up their own company, Yunus Social Business (YSB), in collaboration with the Yunus Centre in Dhaka. They wanted to set up social businesses around the world. They made a beginning by taking over some projects from GCL in Colombia and Haiti.

The objective of YSB is to help build the new economic structure we need by spreading the theory and practice of social business around the world. It engages in several methods. One of them is to serve as a business incubator and a venture fund. This venture fund has one big difference from conventional venture funds. An investment from YSB's venture fund is not made with the objective of earning large profits. As a social business, YSB does not take any profit from the companies in which it makes equity investments. Instead, it takes only a service charge to cover its cost. The concept is simple: YSB's program leaders select the most promising business plans created by local people that are designed to solve local problems in a sustainable way—that is, paying for themselves through revenue-generating activities. Investors are entitled to take back the investment amount. Any profits beyond that will be reinvested into the business or used in some way to benefit the local people. Everything goes back to the community.

Golden Bees in Uganda illustrates YSB's incubator function. The founder of Golden Bees approached YSB's local team seeking advice, support, and funding for his business concept. YSB connected him with local business experts who provided him with free training and guidance on issues such as financial planning and market analysis. Then YSB provided startup investment funds to help Golden Bees get off the ground.

Today YSB's team continues to monitor the growth of Golden Bees and stands ready to provide additional assistance as needed. It is doing the same with more than a dozen other social business startups in Uganda, which are developing businesses such as water purifying systems and improved, environmentally friendly cookstoves.

Since 2011, YSB has grown rapidly. Today, it operates in seven countries—Haiti, Albania, Brazil, Colombia, India, Tunisia, and Uganda. YSB has attracted a strong international team of over forty-five people from diverse backgrounds, all committed to social business. Social businesses that YSB has helped to launch include, for example, Bive, a network of affordable health care providers for the poor in the Caldas region of Colombia; Digo, a business that empowers micro-entrepreneurs to distribute domestic cleaning products to poor people in rural Haiti; and Seniors House, a provider of daycare and residential services for elderly people in Albania.

Beyond its role as a startup incubator, YSB is also working with established for-profit companies that are interested in exploring the possibility of starting social businesses. This model goes back to our joint venture experiences with the successful French corporations Danone and Veolia.

You might wonder why a for-profit company would want to launch a business whose mission is to address a social problem, with no profit-making motive. The reasons vary. In some companies, owners or top executives may feel passionate about a particular problem—poverty, education, health care, pollution, or whatever. They may initiate the idea of starting a social business that will apply their company's expertise to solving that problem. They may also consider this as supportive of company objectives. This initiative may keep their employees engaged and enthusiastic about their work; may earn recognition and praise from the broader community; and may perhaps help them learn more about the social business model and its implications for their business more broadly.

In most cases, however, what motivates business leaders to embrace social business is the same thing that motivates entrepreneurs, students, and others who are fascinated by the concept: they simply care deeply about their fellow human beings and want to do what they can to make life better for them. Social business represents a new economic structure that provides a fresh path for innovation and service. As a result, a growing number of business leaders around the world are excited about experimenting with it.

Sometimes, CEOs and other business executives contact members of the YSB team at their offices in Frankfurt and Berlin, Germany, or in one of their country offices. In other cases, they make a connection with Hans Reitz's team of consultants at the offices of Grameen Creative Lab in Wiesbaden, Germany, or with the experts at the Yunus Centre in Dhaka, Bangladesh, which is the focal point of all my local and international activities. A new office called Yunus Centre Paris will be established in 2017 in the French capital at the request of the city's mayor (more on this later). All of these organizations stand ready to act as clearinghouses and sources of information and guidance about starting a social business—what it is, how it works, and the do's and don'ts of business development.

When appropriate, experts from these organizations provide coaching, training, and consulting to executives who are planning or launching a social business, either as a freestanding company or as a virtual company in a separate division of an existing corporation. They also help leaders of nonprofit agencies or NGOs who are interested in transforming some of their activities into social businesses to address social needs.

The French Action Tank: Tackling
Poverty in a Wealthy Nation

One of the most exciting outgrowths of the burgeoning experimentation that YSB supports has been the creation of what are called Social Business Action Tanks. A play on the term *think tank,* an Action Tank is a gathering of top executives from large corporations who are interested in studying the concept of social business—and then going beyond study to actually launch and build social businesses alongside their mega conventional businesses to address social problems.

The first Social Business Action Tank was founded in Paris in 2010. One of the driving forces behind it was Emmanuel Faber, the man who became CEO of Danone in 2014—a business leader with an imaginative mind, a deeply humane sensibility, and a readiness to experiment with various economic models in search of solutions to humankind's most pressing challenges. Faber and Franck Riboud had already become deeply involved with the social business concept and had launched the first joint venture experiment with it—Grameen Danone Foods in Bangladesh. Seeking to bring this model to Europe, Faber teamed up with Martin Hirsch, a distinguished French social activist and civil servant with long experience in creating programs to help the disadvantaged. They formed a team to bring the Social Business Action Tank into being.

The two men attracted a remarkable set of leaders to the Action Tank, including Jacques Berger, an experienced business consultant who is now director of the Action Tank. Leaders of other businesses soon joined the project. Academic experts from fields like economics and business have signed on to serve as advisers and to study the experiments that were launched, hoping to find lessons that could be used by others.

For example, Bénédicte Faivre-Tavignot, executive director of a special department dedicated to social business at the respected French business school HEC, has been spearheading studies of the work of the Action Tank and sharing her findings with scholars around the world.

As of fall 2016, the French Action Tank—formally known as Action Tank Entreprise et Pauvreté ("business and poverty")—has launched several social businesses, each designed to tackle a serious problem confronting poor people in France.

Helping poor people in a wealthy country involves a different set of challenges than those I've dealt with in Bangladesh, which has been one of the poorest countries on Earth for a long time, or those the YSB team and its entrepreneurial partners have been dealing with in poor nations like Uganda. France is one of the richest nations on Earth. It also has a well-developed social safety net, designed to provide people in need with some of the basic necessities of life—health care, education, a place to live.

Yet France still has a significant share of poor people— an estimated 13 percent of the population, around 8 million people in total. According to Jacques Berger, their numbers steadily declined between 1900 and 1970, but then progress stalled—a typical reflection of the difficulties of reducing poverty in a traditional capitalist system. Some of the French poor are elderly people living on modest, fixed pensions. Others are people who live in rural regions where the economy is foundering. Still others are immigrants from countries in the Middle East, Africa, and Asia, who are searching desperately for a foothold in the French economy.

For these and other people at the bottom of the French social ladder, life is difficult, with numerous barriers that make advancement difficult. The social businesses launched by the

French Action Tank are seeking to reduce or eliminate some of those barriers. The objective is to restart the progress on combating poverty that stalled in 1970, and to move France toward the goal of zero poverty.

One of these social businesses is Mobiliz, a company launched by the automaker Renault, which seeks to bring affordable transportation within reach of poor people. When brainstorming a business model that could support this goal, the managers at Renault considered a number of ideas. For example, they played with the concept of trying to design and build an ultra-low-cost automobile that even the poor could afford. But the more they talked with people in their target market—poor people themselves—the more they realized that this would not solve the most urgent mobility problems these people faced.

Instead, they discovered that many poor people actually owned cars—usually low-quality used cars with lots of years and hundreds of thousands of kilometers on them, which were the best vehicles they could afford to buy. Unfortunately, there is an inverse relationship between the selling price of a car and the cost to maintain it. The old clunkers owned by the poor people of France broke down frequently and were expensive to fix. With their cars constantly at the shop for repairs, they often had to miss work—and when you are a marginal worker with a bottom-of-the-ladder job, missing a couple of days is likely to lead to your being fired.

Renault realized that a key to delivering mobility to the poor people of France was to make auto maintenance and repair affordable to them. So in 2010 they set about building a network of auto repair shops that would agree to serve Mobiliz members at a discount price, while continuing to serve nondiscount clients who allow the shops to fully cover their

costs. There are now several hundred of these "solidarity garages" serving thousands of eligible customers, who have been
identified for Mobiliz by local NGOs that work closely with
the poor. The garages benefit by getting a steady stream of
guaranteed customers who rely on them for auto maintenance
and repair work; the customers benefit from high-quality service that keeps their vehicles on the road, allowing them to
get on with life.

Renault's experiments with social business are not finished. The company is now exploring several other ways of extending mobility services to those who need them, including
affordable and accessible driving classes, using smart phone
technology as one way to bring driver education within reach
of all, and a car-sharing service that will focus on making
low-cost electric vehicles available for hourly rentals in public
housing projects.

Another social business launched through the French Action Tank is Optique Solidaire. This is a separate division of
the French company Essilor, a leading global maker of lenses
and other optical equipment. Many French people are unable
to afford high-quality glasses with progressive lenses, which
typically retail for 230 to 300 euros. A team of experts at Essilor spent fifteen months experimenting with eyeglass designs
and service delivery systems in an effort to drive down this
price. Now they have built a network of more than five hundred retail opticians who can provide high-quality glasses to
those in need for as little as 30 euros. Originally designed to
target elderly customers age sixty and older, the program was
expanded in 2014 to include those in need who are as young
as forty-five. Eligible recipients are those who receive the special form of national health insurance provided to those of
limited means.

Other social business projects created by the Action Tank in collaboration with leading French corporations are now tackling challenges like emergency shelter for the homeless, home insurance for those who can't afford conventional policies, and accessible banking services for the poor.[9]

You can see from these projects that tackling poverty in a wealthy nation of the developed world is rather different from the challenge in a poor country in Asia, Africa, or Latin America. Because the poor are a relatively small fraction of the population who often live in the midst of wealthy neighbors, one of the challenges is finding and identifying them and designing the social business so that its benefits flow to those in need.

I wouldn't want to create an onerous system of tests or rules in an effort to precisely winnow out any "undeserving" participants. But I want to ensure that a social business whose goal is to alleviate the effects of poverty does in fact serve that goal. Making the service or product open to all at the same price may crowd out those most in need. This is why the Action Tank's experiments in targeting the poor are important.

The projects created by the French Action Tank have proven to be so exciting and successful that the concept is now spreading to other countries. YSB is now in the process of launching Action Tanks in India and Brazil. These two countries are in a very different economic situation than France. Both are developing nations with a rapidly growing middle class and a very large, persistent population of poor people, both in the countryside and in vast urban slums. Both countries also have some very large companies with global reach. I suspect that some of the ideas that will emerge from these two new Action Tanks may resemble those we see in France, while others will be quite different, tailored to the needs of a different social structure.

In both India and Brazil, the YSB teams have already received commitments from a series of corporate participants who are eager to experiment with new economic structures. They've also established connections with local universities that will provide research support. It will be fascinating to watch these new experiments unfold. Similar initiatives are now taking shape in Japan and Australia. Action Tanks do not have to be limited to rich countries or big countries. They can be created in poor countries and small countries as well, involving local and multinational companies that operate there. Eventually, we should be able to use the lessons from these countries to help us design Social Business Action Tanks for many other cities in every region of the world.

The New Economy and the Goal of Zero Poverty

As these examples suggest, the economic transformation that social business is helping to jump-start gives humankind for the first time the opportunity to create a world without poverty.

I am energized by the conviction that poverty is not created by poor people. Poverty is an artificial imposition on people who are endowed with the same unlimited potential for creativity and energy of any human being in any station of life, anywhere in the world. Eliminating poverty is a question of removing the barriers faced by poor people to unleash their creativity to solve their problems. They can change their lives, if we only give them the same opportunities that the rest of us have.

Creatively designed social businesses in all sectors can make this happen in the fastest way. I always insist that poverty does not belong in civilized society. Poverty belongs only in museums where our children and grandchildren will go to see what inhumanity people had to suffer, and where they will ask themselves how their ancestors allowed such a condition to persist for so long.

The rising generation has the power to ensure the elimination of poverty from this planet. We overcame slavery, we overcame apartheid, we put human beings on the moon—all achievements that were once considered impossible. We can overcome poverty, if we only decide that poverty does not belong to the future that we want to create. It is up to us to decide that the world we choose to live in will not contain the scourge of poverty—and then to create the new economic system that will make the world we choose possible.

4

ZERO UNEMPLOYMENT:
WE ARE NOT JOB SEEKERS,
WE ARE JOB CREATORS

SINCE THE GREAT RECESSION OF 2008–2009, people around the world have developed a deepening sense that something is terribly wrong with our economic system. Youth unemployment is a particularly striking part of the story. In Europe, unemployment among people under age twenty-five is at 18.6 percent (as of December 2016). In some countries, including Greece, Spain, and Italy, the rate is over 40 percent.[1] And in the United States, a significant number of young people have become discouraged and dropped out of the workforce, leading to rosier unemployment statistics that understate the scope of the real problem.[2]

Furthermore, research shows that youth unemployment isn't a temporary problem. Young people who spend several years without work, or working in low-paying jobs with no growth prospects, suffer lifelong consequences. No matter how hard they work, they are unlikely to ever make their way

onto the fast track of jobs that pay well, provide lifetime security, and create opportunities for the next generation.

The blights of unemployment and underemployment help
determine an individual's lifetime income and are two major
contributing factors to the rise of economic inequality, which,
as I've observed, poses a serious threat to the future of the
world. The psychological and social impact is just as severe.
Unemployment means throwing a fully capable person into
the trash—a particularly cruel form of punishment.

A human being is born to be active, creative, energetic,
and a problem solver, always seeking new ways to unleash his
or her unlimited potential. Why should we allow anybody to
unplug a creative human being and deny that person the opportunity to use his or her amazing capacities? Yet today, I
see millions of young people in the United States and Europe
being pushed into forced idleness thanks to a massive failure
of the economic system. As a result, a generation of young
people is burdened with a sense of hopelessness.

In my visits with young people throughout the world, I've
encountered endless numbers of bright, energetic women and
men who feel stranded by the limitations of today's economy
and our flawed policies. Unemployed or underemployed, they
can't afford to buy homes or start families—much less to repay the tens of thousands of dollars in student loans they often carry. They wonder what they have done wrong and why
the world seems to have no use for their talents. No wonder
economists like Spain's Ludovic Subran have lamented, "An
entire generation is being sacrificed."[3]

Making matters worse, demographic and economic trends
show no sign of solving this problem automatically. The International Labour Organization (ILO) estimates that the
labor force will grow through the addition of young people

by a total of about 400 million people in the next decade. This adds up to what the ILO calls the "urgent challenge" of creating 400 million productive jobs over the next decade— 40 million jobs per year.[4]

The problem is made worse by trends such as automation, the spread of robotic technology, and advances in artificial intelligence, all of which are making it possible for companies to eliminate workers in many fields without diminishing output. In addition, people are living longer, healthier lives, which means they both want and need to work longer to support themselves, putting additional pressure on the employment rolls. It seems likely that in the years to come, politicians and governments will become more and more overwhelmed by the issues of job creation and unemployment management.

What is the cause of this problem? What can we do to fix it?

THE PROBLEM OF UNEMPLOYMENT— WRONG DIAGNOSIS, WRONG CURE

OF COURSE, TODAY'S YOUNG PEOPLE who are struggling to find decent jobs have done nothing wrong—just as the poor women around the world who are trapped in poverty have done nothing wrong. In both cases, the economic system that we designed and have been following with total trust is to blame—and that needs to change.

This problem of unemployment is not created by the unemployed people themselves. It is created by our grossly flawed conceptual framework, which has drilled into our heads that people are born to work for a few fortunate capitalists. Since these few job creators are the drivers of the economy, according to the present theory, all policies and institutions are built for them. If they don't hire you, you are finished. What a misreading of human destiny! What an insult to human beings who are packed with unlimited creative capacity!

Our education system reflects this same economic theory. It is built on the assumption that students should work hard and get good grades so that they can get good jobs from the corporations that are assumed to be the drivers of all economic activity and growth. The world's top universities pride themselves on the extent to which their graduates appear at the graduation ceremony with appointment letters in their pockets.

There's nothing wrong with people working for a company for all their lives, or part of their lives. But there's something very wrong with an economic system that blindly ignores the existence of a natural and attractive alternative. Young people are never told that they are all born with two choices, and that they continue to have these two choices throughout their lives: they can be job seekers or job creators—entrepreneurs in their own right rather than relying on the favor of a job from other entrepreneurs.

We cannot just sit and watch a whole generation of young people fall through the cracks of economic theory because we are too timid to question the wisdom of our theoreticians. We have to redesign our theory by recognizing the limitless capacity of a human being, instead of relying on the "invisible hand of the market" to solve all our problems. We have to wake up to the fact that the "invisible hand" is invisible because it does not exist—or, if it does exist, it is dedicated to serving the rich, invisibly.

In the current economic system, theoreticians have never offered us any better solutions for unemployment than promoting economic growth through investments in infrastructure building or make-work government programs, along with state charity designed to alleviate the suffering of those in need. These policies can provide partial solutions to the problem, but they fail to address the real, underlying issue.

Of course, when people are hurting because of unemployment, government help to relieve them is necessary and important. But immediately after that, the much higher responsibility of society—and of the state that represents it—is to help people escape dependence on the state as soon as possible. Dependence diminishes human beings. Our mission on this planet is to make it a better place for everybody—not to tolerate the existence of a dependent underclass without the freedom and independence that make life truly worth living.

We have the technology and the economic methodology needed to bring an end to the scourge of unemployment. All that is lacking is a framework and the will.

OVERCOMING BARRIERS TO WORK

ONE OF THE MYTHS THAT feeds the unemployment problem is the idea that some people are incapable of producing economic value. These people supposedly have flaws or failings that make them worthless and deserving of being discarded like so much trash. The myth says they are fit only to receive charity or government handouts.

Some people need help in overcoming barriers that make it harder for them to do worthwhile work. Some have physical or psychological disabilities that require some support—for example, special tools or machines adapted to their circumstances, or modified work schedules suitable for their conditions. Some workers whose jobs have been eliminated due to automation need training to help them develop new skills. Problems like these should never have been allowed to create a large, permanent class of unemployed people like that we see in most countries around the world.

The reality is that almost all human beings are perfectly capable of doing worthwhile work that contributes value to society while letting them support themselves and their families—especially when they are freed from the demand of generating large, ever-growing profits for a corporate master. Today there are social businesses demonstrating that this is true. One example is Human Harbor Corporation, established in Fukuoka, Japan, in December 2012.

I first heard about Human Harbor during a visit to Kyushu University in 2012, when a social business design competition was held by the university's Yunus & Shiiki Social Business Research Center. One of the most promising designs was presented by Isao Soejima, who was working as a prison probation officer. Soejima was troubled by the plight of ex-prisoners, who face serious obstacles in finding work after they are released from prison—obstacles mostly created by society itself. Excluded from ordinary jobs by fear and prejudice, many return to crime, using contacts in the underworld that they established while in prison. Like most countries, Japan must cope with a high percentage of ex-prisoners who wind up back in prison after committing fresh crimes; statistics show that the national recidivism rate has recently risen from around 30 percent to over 46 percent.[5]

Soejima wanted to create a social business to address this problem. In partnership with an ex-prisoner named Atsushi Takayama, he founded Human Harbor Corporation (HH), the first Yunus Social Business in Japan. HH tackles two social problems: it collects and recycles industrial waste, thereby reducing the problem of pollution and environmental damage, and in the process it employs a number of supposedly "unemployable" people recently released from prison.

Soejima's business plan has been working. HH quickly became self-sustaining, reaching revenues of US$2.4 million in 2016 and aiming for revenues of US$3.5 million in 2017. The company employs twenty-six people, nine of them ex-prisoners, in three locations—Fukuoka, Tokyo, and Osaka. One of HH's employees, Taro Tachibana, left the company in 2015 to start his own waste recycling social business in partnership with HH. Thus, the idea behind HH is already spreading and expanding naturally, the way successful business concepts tend to do.

Companies like HH expose the idea that any group of people is incapable of useful work as a myth we need to reject. It is simply one of the old ideas that operates as a barrier to creating a new economic system in which every human being can find a place.

Tackling Unemployment in Bangladesh: The Nobin (New Entrepreneurs) Program

For years, I was troubled by the problem of rampant unemployment among the second generation of Grameen borrowers. This new generation had gone to school; many had even enjoyed higher education. Still, many thousands of them could not find jobs.

Finally, I went ahead with my solution. It is a practical solution to the unemployment problem that opens the doors of economic opportunity for young people in Bangladesh.

As I've explained, Grameen Bank and the financial system known as microcredit started out with a tiny initiative in the village of Jobra in 1976. Microcredit has since grown into a worldwide movement that has helped over 300 million poor families improve their economic circumstances through entrepreneurship.

Right from the beginning, Grameen Bank paid attention to some basic issues regarding the poor, paying attention to their awareness of important practices like simple hygiene and proper health care. We supported good lifestyle choices like the habit of saving by making it easy for Grameen borrowers to make deposits into savings accounts.

We also focused intensely on the second generation in the families of borrowers. We encouraged Grameen families to use the meeting place known as Centre House—a hut in which borrowers assemble to hold their weekly meetings—as a place of learning for their children. Many local borrowers' groups would pay a local girl or woman a modest salary (usually around 500 *taka*, the equivalent of about six US dollars), to teach their preschool kids every day. These new neighborhood centers for fun and learning have introduced countless kids to reading and writing, and helped families that might never have experienced classroom learning to overcome their fears about education and instead to embrace it.

We also included the commitment of sending every child to school in the basic charter of pledges of the borrowers, famously known as the Sixteen Decisions. These commitments—including number seven, "We shall educate our children and ensure that they can earn to pay for their education"—are chanted by all Grameen Bank borrowers collectively, in every center meeting, week after week, year after year. We launched a campaign to make sure that 100 percent of the children of Grameen families go to school—a daring effort in a country where most children of poor families do not go to school—and we gave scholarships to thousands of students each year to encourage them to continue in school and compete for better performance.

When they finished primary school, we encouraged them to go to high school. Most of them did. And when they finished high school, we encouraged them to go to college, introducing a new program of education loans to make higher education available to children from poor village families. Now thousands of students have taken education loans from Grameen Bank to become graduates, doctors, engineers, and professional people.

But this achievement led to a new problem. For most of the new graduates, there are no jobs. So we launched another program. It started with a campaign to redirect the minds of young people from the traditional path of hunting for jobs to one of creating jobs for themselves and others through entrepreneurship. We invited children from Grameen families to repeat the mantra, "We are not job seekers, we are job creators." And to help them turn this belief into a reality, we introduced a new program of offering new-entrepreneur loans from Grameen Bank to support their efforts to create businesses. We started calling the young people who choose that path *nobin udyokta,* which means "new entrepreneurs" in our Bangla language.

When we first announced the Nobin program in 2001, the volume of businesses launched was small. Many Grameen parents were reluctant to let their sons or daughters take more loans while they still had outstanding education loans to repay. Moreover, some Grameen bank staffers were very slow in giving them fresh loans because of the same concern about outstanding loans.

To help remedy this problem and to encourage more Grameen youth to embrace entrepreneurship, I came up with the idea of creating social business funds outside the Grameen

Bank structure to take sole responsibility for financing new entrepreneurs. To implant the ideas of entrepreneurship in the minds of all the stakeholders and to refine the methodology through regular interaction with people from all walks of life, I decided to create an open platform where potential young entrepreneurs could present their business designs. I was hoping that the existence of this platform would encourage young people to come up with business ideas while helping to demonstrate how social business concepts can be applied to concrete social and economic challenges.

In January 2013, the Yunus Centre in Dhaka organized the first Social Business Design Lab. Encouraged by its success, we decided to hold monthly Design Labs. They attract business executives, NGO leaders, academics, students, subject specialists, and social activists. Sometimes participants offer to become investors in projects presented at the lab.

By April 2017, nearly sixteen thousand new entrepreneurs had their business plans approved and received advice and guidance as well as US$21 million in investment funding through the Social Business Design Labs. Although public Design Labs are still held monthly, many more in-house Design Labs are held to bring about one thousand business plans per month to the final approval level. By the end of 2017, the number of business plans approved for funding may reach two thousand per month. So far, we have maintained very high quality in our selection and monitoring. Although we are trying to go slowly to ensure quality, we expect to reach 25,000 project approvals with US$36 million invested in them by the end of 2017.

Note that the funds and investors that invest in the new entrepreneurs are social businesses, but the new entrepreneurs themselves establish conventional businesses that are dedicated to making profits for the owners. To give you a feeling for the kinds of business ideas that are being funded through the Nobin program, here are six approved projects from a Design Lab in May 2016:

- Mitali Tailors—A young widow and mother of two named Rumi Mallik received funding to help expand her late husband's tailoring business some eight months after his death.
- Priyonto Nursery—An expert at plant propagation using the grafting method, Ranjan Chandra Sutradhar received an investment to help him launch his own nursery business.
- Etee Jamdani House—Mussamat Parvin, a skilled weaver of *jamdani,* a fine muslin sari textile, received funds to expand her home-based company.
- Salim Pakha Shilpo—Asma Begum, who was compelled to leave her husband after suffering physical torture, received funds to help her launch a business making traditional palm-leaf hand fans.
- Tumpa Rice Mill—Muhammad Ruhul Amin, an experienced rice mill operator, got funds to create his own rice mill business.
- Bodhua Beauty Parlor—Trained beautician Hasna Begun received funding to expand her business.

As you can see, these are not giant projects like those favored by many traditional economic development programs—steel mills, electronics factories, hydroelectric plants. Rather, they are small, bottom-up companies designed by local young people who understand community needs and preferences, each requiring funding in the range of US$1,000 to

US$3,000. Each of these businesses will start with the entre-
preneur alone, who will then hire one or more extra hands as
expansion takes place. Yet each represents an opportunity for a
youth to get a first taste of the excitement of entrepreneurship
and independence while providing a useful good or service to
the community. Multiplied by the thousands and eventually
by the millions, entrepreneurial businesses like these can help
to revitalize the economies of countless rural villages in Bangladesh and transform the prospects of our youth.

It took the Yunus Centre some time to work out today's
successful system for operating the Nobin program. Between
January and September 2013, we developed the basic methodology, reporting formats, daily monitoring system, accounting
procedures, identification and assessment procedures, and so
on. Now common facilities such as computerized management information systems, accounting software, and training facilities are being developed. A rigorous implementation
structure is emerging to make sure that the new entrepreneurs
get a thorough orientation and training in business management, accounting, and reporting, as well as access to support
services.

Initially, Grameen Telecom Trust—a member of the
Grameen family of businesses—was the main investor providing funds for the new entrepreneurs. Now more Grameen
companies, including Grameen Kalyan (a health care company), Grameen Shakti Samajik Bybosha (dedicated to
business promotion), and Grameen Trust (dedicated to international replication of the Grameen methodology) have
joined the program. Together they have created a total of four
social business funds to carry out their own Nobin programs.

Typically around 150 people attend each publicly held
monthly Design Lab, while others in over thirty countries

take part in the session as it is live-streamed via the Internet. Participants ask questions, suggest ways to improve the project, and raise issues that may have been missed in the project preparation.

The Design Lab itself is actually the culmination of an elaborate process that begins with the identification of a potential new entrepreneur. Each social business fund has its own village level office with staff to seek out aspiring entrepreneurs, to keep in close contact with them, and to help them solve their problems. They visit would-be entrepreneurs in their homes to learn more about their dreams, their worries, and their family support. Once thirty to fifty young men and women have been identified and contacted, the village staff will organize an orientation camp. There they explain the rules and procedures of the New Entrepreneur program, invite each participant to briefly explain his or her business concept, and lead a joint discussion and evaluation of each idea. Afterward, the camp leaders make a short list of the participants who have impressed them as entrepreneurs likely to succeed—the first step in the selection process.

Does this mean that those who fail to make the cut are doomed to unemployment? Not at all. We explain our basic policy to all participants: nobody is rejected, and nobody is abandoned even if his or her project initially fails. We follow this policy all through the process. So those who are not selected for the program the first time are assured that they will be invited to the next camp. Meanwhile, they can prepare themselves to make a better project presentation next time.

The short-listed candidates go through a second round of project development exercises. Entrepreneurs selected in this round are invited to Dhaka, where they'll give their business plans a final shape and a professional appearance with the help of trained investor staff. Project summaries are prepared in English for a five-minute presentation at the Design Lab.

Usually, after this long process of preparation, the Design Lab judges are happy to approve each project, though they often give some good advice and flag some issues to help improve the real-world implementation of the business plan. In rare cases, an entrepreneur is asked to modify his or her plan to make further improvement and present it at the next Design Lab.

Once the project is approved, the hand-holding process for implementation begins. The investor and the entrepreneur go through a period of training and mentoring for a successful shared journey. Along with the investment, the fledgling entrepreneur is given management training, coaching, and advice to help ensure the success of the new business. This is only natural, since the investors have a strong social interest in the success of the business. So just as venture capitalists provide coaching and advice to maximize the growth potential of the businesses they support, our social business investors offer help and guidance to the new companies they are backing.

During this period, any regulatory issues related to the proposed business are thrashed out, and all necessary documentation is completed. Monitoring and accounting training are completed.

Finally, the investment funds are released, and the business starts rolling. Accounting and monitoring software developed by Grameen Communication (an information technology company that is part of the Grameen family of businesses) gathers key data from every new entrepreneur's business on a daily basis. All these reports go to a central server, which generates daily monitoring reports for all businesses and presents the data via user-friendly dashboards provided to the investing funds.

The Nobin program is firmly based on the conviction that everyone has the potential to become an entrepreneur—to take care of his or her life as well as to contribute to the economy and society by creating a business based on individual creativity. By bringing together social business funds, investors, experts in business design, and would-be youth entrepreneurs who need capital and support, we are demonstrating the truth of that conviction—and helping thousands of low-income youth escape the trap of unemployment.

From Loans to Equity: Key to Promoting Entrepreneurship

When I was promoting microcredit for poor women in the early years of Grameen Bank, many experts around the world insisted that the concept would fail because entrepreneurship is a rare quality in people—and even rarer in poor people, and extremely rare among poor women. I took the reverse position—that all human beings are entrepreneurs, with no exceptions, men or women, rural or urban, rich or poor. The Nobin program has its roots in the same firm belief.

One big difference between microcredit and the Nobin program is that the latter focuses on providing would-be business builders with equity financing—that is, investment funding—rather than loans. Let me take a moment to explain how equity financing works in the world of social business.

In the social business version of venture capital, investors do not take any profit from their investment. However, they get their investment money back, plus a sum we refer to as a *share transfer fee,* which equals 20 percent of the total investment—no more. So in the Nobin program, entrepreneurs are responsible for paying back whatever money they received, along with the share transfer fee, within an agreed period. When this happens, ownership of the company is transferred to the entrepreneur.

Having a share transfer fee fixed at 20 percent avoids the need for assessing the share value at the time of ownership transfer. Looking at it from a different perspective, this 20 percent fee may be seen as a modest compensation for all the training, hand-holding, consultancy services, problem-solving services, and accounting services each business received since the new entrepreneur and the investor began working together. It also provides money to cover the management costs of the social business fund itself. With this fee, we believe that our social business funds will be able to support themselves as sustainable businesses that can continue to help turn unemployed young people into entrepreneurs.

The share transfer fee does all this at a relatively small cost. If the entrepreneur had borrowed the money from a bank in Bangladesh, his or her interest burden would have grown at least twice as much in a three-year repayment period as the 20 percent we designate. If the repayment period had been longer, the interest amount would have been several times as much. All in all, I think that charging a share transfer fee when the entrepreneur takes ownership of the business is a reasonable way of covering the costs associated with providing financing for a new business venture.

I am convinced that the potential of programs like the Nobin program is enormous. This concept offers the possibility of addressing the issue of youth unemployment—or any unemployment, for that matter—in a sustainable and a replicable way. It shifts the agenda from the traditional formula of job creation through profit-maximizing corporate initiatives or investments in large infrastructure projects by governments to simple, sustainable, and direct microequity financing of a business conceived by the unemployed person. Here our action directly aims at the person whose problem is to be solved. The solution is no longer the uncertain by-product of an enterprise designed for a very different purpose—namely, a business built to maximize profits for somebody else.

Like Grameen Bank, the Nobin program has developed a robust methodology. It can be applied in any country, any corner of any city, any village, or any community. It is self-contained and financially self-reliant. It can be applied wherever unemployment or underemployment exists, in crowded cities or thinly populated villages, in refugee camps or among immigrant communities, and in low-income countries or very rich countries. It works because the basic context is the same everywhere—all human beings are born entrepreneurs.

The methodology of the Nobin program is relatively easy to apply on a large scale, as we are doing in Bangladesh, or on the smallest scale imaginable—one unemployed person at a time. Any individual with money to invest can apply it to tackling unemployment in a community of his or her choice. Simply evaluate the business idea floated by a would-be entrepreneur; offer advice, counseling, and support to improve the success chances of the fledgling business; and provide equity funding of an agreed amount to be repaid by the entrepreneur during a fixed period of time. A share transfer fee of 20 percent should be included, which formalizes the transfer of ownership in the business from the investor to the entrepreneur.

In the case of an individual social business investor who wants to invest in two or three new entrepreneurs, what happens to the equity funding once the entrepreneurs repay it? Having received the original money back, a social business investor can choose to do whatever he or she wants with it:

reinvest the money in the next new entrepreneur, or use it for whatever purpose he or she prefers.

An investor who does reinvest the money in another entrepreneur will be demonstrating the potential power of the new economic model to the fullest possible extent. Unlike a charity dollar, a social business dollar that is reinvested never gets used up. Instead, it keeps working, helping to lift one person after another out of joblessness, bringing the day of zero unemployment steadily closer.

From the Villages of Bangladesh to the Streets of New York: Microcredit as a Tool for Promoting Entrepreneurship

Even in the wealthiest countries on Earth, large numbers of people are stuck in poverty or near-poverty because they are forced to rely on job opportunities as the only possible source of income. Much of the economic distress in countries like the United States—distress that helped to fuel the rising tide of anger, frustration, and hostility that led to the startling 2016 election victory of Donald Trump—can be traced to the fact that people are trapped in a system that relies on big employers to keep local economies flourishing. Thus, when big companies move overseas, automate their plants, or shut down altogether, entire communities can be destroyed. And in neighborhoods dominated by members of disfavored groups who are last in line for jobs—groups like people of color—unemployment can become a permanent condition, condemning generations to lives of struggle and suffering.

I believe the entrepreneurial solution can play a big role in alleviating this problem in the United States and in other wealthy countries, just as it is beginning to do in Bangladesh. For evidence, I point to the rising success of Grameen America, the bank that has brought the methods and philosophy of Grameen Bank from Bangladesh to cities across the United States.

For decades, people have wondered whether microcredit could empower poor people and alleviate the harm caused by unemployment in wealthy nations. This is one of the reasons government and business leaders from around the world have been studying Grameen Bank and seeking to learn from it. The first replication of Grameen Bank in the United States took place in 1987 in Arkansas, one of the poorer states in the nation. It's how I became friends with Hillary Rodham Clinton when she was First Lady of Arkansas, long before she lived in the White House and served as a US senator and secretary of state.

Since then, despite the Arkansas experience, many people had argued that Grameen-style programs could not survive in the United States, since the people and the economy are so different from those in Bangladesh. I continued to disagree strongly. Some urged me to demonstrate my views through an actual program in the United States. I finally took the plunge in 2008. With financial and management support from Vidar Jorgensen, a committed entrepreneur from Massachusetts, we launched Grameen America, Inc. (GAI) starting with a single branch in the neighborhood of Jackson Heights in the borough of Queens in New York City.

The response was immediate and positive. Many local women of diverse backgrounds were excited to learn about the possibility of getting access to credit that would enable them to start their own businesses or expand the tiny businesses they already owned. Just as in Bangladesh, GAI's client base consists of women who would never have been considered creditworthy by a conventional bank—women with no collateral, no assets, no savings, no references. All they had was an idea and a strong desire to work hard to make it succeed.

Within months, GAI's Jackson Heights branch had recruited hundreds of members, as they are called. As it became a successful program, requests began to flood the GAI office from cities around the United States that wanted GAI to bring their services to them. However, finding that funds to start these programs were not easily available, GAI's leaders decided to move slowly, making sure that adequate funding was in place before launching any new branch. They also wanted to make sure they didn't risk an overaccelerated expansion, which could stretch their human resources and management capabilities too thin. They were thoughtful about choosing locations where they felt the need was real and where local financial support was strong.

GAI is now led by Andrea Jung, former president and CEO of Avon. Her dedicated work has given GAI a robust, financially sustainable organizational framework. As of March 2017, GAI works through nineteen branches in twelve cities, including New York; Los Angeles; Indianapolis; Omaha; and Charlotte, North Carolina. They have over eighty-six thousand members, all of them women, many of them undocumented immigrants whose status often makes it difficult for them to access mainstream social and financial services. GAI members have received loans totaling more than US$590 million, and they maintain a repayment rate of over 99 percent.

Next year, GAI will celebrate its tenth anniversary, by which time it projects a membership of more than one hundred thousand and a cumulative total of more than a billion dollars in loans. In the next decade, Jung hopes to reach a million borrowers through a network of 100 branches. This will require about US$1.5 billion in loans and equity, a sum that can easily be raised if GAI can get a limited banking license allowing it to accept deposits or if GAI launches a social business fund to raise capital.

One of the crucial lessons of GAI lies in the fact that the operating principles and systems that make microcredit successful in places like New York and Nebraska are almost precisely the same as those we developed for use in the villages of Bangladesh. We lend to a woman only after she forms a group of five or joins a group that is under construction. The women in the group offer one another mutual support, advice, and encouragement. Before receiving a loan, a member must present GAI staff with a business idea and a plausible plan for carrying it out successfully. Members also commit to keeping their children in school, nurturing the health and well-being of their families, and otherwise building toward a better future. In all these ways, the Grameen microcredit formula in the United States is exactly the same as in Bangladesh.

It's important to understand that not all of the organizations around the world that have jumped on the microcredit bandwagon have followed the same consistent rules. Many NGOs have launched microcredit programs that ignore or twist the principles that made Grameen Bank successful and effective. Most egregiously, some have converted microcredit from a social business dedicated to helping poor people (and, in the case of Grameen Bank, actually owned and controlled by the poor people themselves) into a money-making scheme designed to enrich the affluent by making profits off the poor.

One result has been so-called microcredit companies that charge interest rates of 80 percent or more, several times the maximum rate charged by Grameen Bank. They justify these exorbitant rates by pointing to the challenges of servicing poor people and the risks of nonrepayment. But Grameen Bank has dealt with these same challenges while making sure that the poor can keep and use most of the money they earn from their businesses, rather than having to pay it to Grameen Bank as the cost of their loans.

Other microcredit organizations insist on collateral for loans—property that the borrowers pledge to guarantee their debt. This practice excludes the world's poorest people, the very ones I designed microcredit to help. In other cases, companies selling nonessential consumer products lure poor people to buy them by arranging finance through so-called microcredit programs. This is completely contrary to the Grameen purpose. We lend money to support productive investments so that the borrowers can build assets and lift themselves and their families out of poverty. Excessive borrowing for consumption tends to mire people in debt and traps them more firmly in the chains of poverty rather than liberating them.

For all these reasons, I urge people who want to understand how microcredit really works to study the Grameen organizations, including the Grameen Bank in Bangladesh, GAI in the United States, and many others around the world. I strongly condemn microcredit programs that are designed to make money for their rich owners. They are a distortion of the model we created to help the poor to overcome poverty, which abuses the concept of microcredit and confuses the world about the purpose of microcredit.

Of course, economic and social conditions in Bangladesh and the United States are very different. So are some of the market circumstances in which the two programs operate. For example, in Bangladesh, Grameen Bank works in rural villages, which is where most of the poor in the country are concentrated. In the United States, poverty is found in both rural and urban areas, but so far GAI branches have been opened only in inner-city locations. That means the kinds of small businesses GAI helps to support are ones designed to succeed in urban settings, serving an urban customer base.

In addition, the investment needed to start a business is typically much larger in the United States than it is in Bangladesh, so the size of an average loan is much greater. In Bangladesh, many women are able to start a business with a loan valued at just forty to fifty dollars—enough to buy a sewing machine, a hand loom, or some simple products to open a small village shop. In the United States, GAI's startup loans typically run between US$1,000 and US$1,500. As members repay their initial loans and build their businesses, they become eligible for further loans that are usually for larger amounts.

Here are a few examples of successful entrepreneurs that GAI has helped to support through loans:

- Damaris M. joined GAI in 2014 and used her first loan of US$1,500 to buy supplies for her new restaurant in Boston, Sabor de Mi Tierra, where she serves specialty Caribbean and Central American foods. Three years later, she is on her sixth loan and has expanded her business with a cumulative total of over US$17,000 in loans. Damaris has one part-time employee and is helped in meeting the growing demand by her son Brian, who manages early-morning shopping runs, and her daughter Diana, who is in charge of deliveries.
- Reyna H., a mother of seven, looks to entrepreneurship as a way of providing for her children and setting an example of how hard work can pay off. In 2015, she joined GAI, borrowing US$1,500 to buy

paint, merchandise, display shelves, and jewelry cases for her storefront boutique in North Austin, Texas. Now on her third loan, Reyna has added technology to let her accept credit card payments and is hoping to expand into a larger storefront closer to her customers in downtown Austin.

- Greisy N. has owned her beauty salon for over fifteen years but lacked the resources needed to expand the shop and keep up with growing demand. In 2016, she joined GAI's branch in Newark, New Jersey, and received a loan of US$1,300 that she used to buy hair dye and other beauty products. She has also opened a free savings account and is setting aside a portion of her income every week in the hopes of making long overdue renovations to her shop.

STORIES LIKE THESE ILLUSTRATE THE fact that the lending system we developed for poor people in the rural villages of Bangladesh works equally well for underprivileged people in the streets of the United States. The adjustments needed to replicate the program in America have proven to be extremely superficial. It turns out that the fundamental characteristics of human beings—including, most important, their potential for entrepreneurial talent—are the same in all countries and among all ethnic groups. This gives me hope that a method to fix unemployment that works in one place can eventually work everywhere.

Now that GAI has been established on a firm foothold, the next natural step will be to develop a Nobin program to invest in businesses launched by low-income American youth. We're making plans for such a program, and I hope we will be able to launch it soon.

ENTREPRENEURSHIP, THE NEW ECONOMY,
AND THE GOAL OF ZERO UNEMPLOYMENT

FOR MANY READERS, THE STORY I've told in this chapter probably seems paradoxical. Many people, including many economists, consider the United States the most dynamic and innovative capitalist nation in history—and therefore the model of an entrepreneurial economy. Yet this stronghold of free-market dynamism has long been plagued by the seemingly insurmountable problem of unemployment, which condemns millions of people to idleness.

The intractable nature of this problem has even driven economists to invent the self-contradicting concept of "full employment." This does not refer to full employment at all but rather to some vaguely defined minimum level of unemployment—perhaps 4 or 5 percent—that leaves an "acceptable" number of millions of people on the scrap heap. That term tells the world not only that it is okay to leave millions unemployed, but that you are lucky to get away with such an insignificant number!

The Grameen Bank experience made me bold enough to challenge this doctrine of despair. I realized that when we open up the gateway to money for people who are trapped in idleness, we can rescue them from all their helplessness. They can do anything they want. Their minds can wake up. A job recruiter's yes or no will no longer decide their fate. They do not have to be at the mercy of others.

It is interesting to note that my idea of turning unemployed people into entrepreneurs originated in a country that was almost exclusively a country of petty farmers until forty years ago. Now I am urging the highly industrialized West to adopt this idea to solve the problem of unemployment, particularly youth unemployment. If this happens, it will be a reversal of the usual pattern whereby new ideas get invented in the West and then gradually find their way to the Global South. I hope my friends in the wealthy nations will not hesitate to apply the idea merely because it is coming from an unlikely country.

If we can turn unemployment into entrepreneurship, the amount of human creativity, talent, and productivity we will unleash is almost beyond measuring. Even more important, we can save hundreds of millions of people from state dependency and the unhappiness human beings suffer when they have been deemed unnecessary and useless.

This will have several vital impacts on the ever-increasing process of wealth concentration. First, each new microentrepreneur we launch will become a microfocus of wealth gathering. The portion of wealth the entrepreneur amasses will be stopped from flowing to the top 1, 2, or 5 percent. Little by little, new pockets of wealth will develop that can help generate prosperity in communities where the 1 percent never set foot.

Second, the top 1 percent will find they have fewer people at their service. All the micro-entrepreneurs who are busy running their own businesses will no longer be available to work for the 1 percent as mercenaries. To that extent, the wealth flow toward the top will slow down.

Third, the spread of entrepreneurship will enable women to participate more fully in the economy—a problem in both the developing nations and the wealthy nations of the world. In today's job-seeking world, women are seriously disadvantaged. Most jobs do not suit them. Rigid workplace rules conflict with the roles many women want to play as mothers and as the central pillars of family life. Efforts to adjust the rules as an afterthought to make jobs more female-friendly have been only partially successful. As a result, millions of women feel as if they have been forced out of the workplace, and the world is deprived of their creativity and participation.

In a world of universal entrepreneurship, women can design their work lives as they wish, using technology to work when they want and from wherever they want. Aspects of the economy not known to men will be revealed by women, and the fresh engagement of millions of women will give productivity a significant boost.

As a result of these changes, the spread of entrepreneurship will accelerate economic growth. Rather than relying on a few mega drivers of the economy to stimulate growth and job creation, universal entrepreneurship will make growth and job creation faster. It will raise incomes and consumption levels among ordinary people and thereby dramatically expand the economy—far more so than trying to sell a few more luxury goods to a handful of wealthy people who already have more things than they will ever need.

Hopefully, in the years to come, the new economic system we are creating will cause the current unidirectional flow of wealth to the top to halt or even reverse itself, and the dream of an egalitarian world will become a reality. The current reliance on government-provided welfare benefits or private charity will give way to a new system in which anyone can take advantage of the opportunities provided by the free market to support his or her family as well as to contribute to the progress of society.

This may seem like an impossible goal. But now we can realize that it is not. Its achievement is blocked only by our own lack of proper understanding of human capabilities.

Viewed through this new lens, the problem identified by the ILO of finding work for 40 million young people every year appears very different. Rather than seeing 40 million young people waiting in line to fill out job applications, I see 40 million new entrepreneurs entering the global market, creating new businesses, solving problems, rejuvenating and reshaping communities, and giving the economy a big boost. Over time, I see the prospects for a shortage of labor, not an excess of labor. Young people, old people, women, people with disabilities—all will flood the market with creative talent and entrepreneurial surprises. Employment bureaus will no longer be charged with finding jobs for people; instead, they'll face the challenges of trying to persuade people to be willing to work for others.

All we need to do is change the economic system—which starts with challenging the orthodoxy that currently controls it.

5

ZERO NET CARBON: CREATING AN ECONOMICS OF SUSTAINABILITY

B ECAUSE I HAVE LIVED MY entire life in Bangladesh, not
so long ago one of the poorest nations in the world, it is
probably obvious why I have developed a deep interest in and
concern about the problems of poverty and unemployment.
My reasons for being equally concerned about the global environment may not be so obvious. But Bangladesh is also one
of the most environmentally vulnerable countries on Earth.
By many accounts, it is ground zero for the devastating future
impact of climate change.

If you are like most Americans, you may find it difficult
to locate Bangladesh on a world map. It is a small country
in the northeastern part of South Asia, largely surrounded by
two giant neighbors that are rapidly increasing in population,
wealth, and power—India and China. But though it is a small
country, Bangladesh has one of the world's largest populations.
In fact, with 165 million people, it is the ninth most populous

nation on Earth. Combined with its small size—at 143,000 square kilometers, Bangladesh is a little smaller in area than the US state of Iowa—this makes Bangladesh one of the most densely populated nations on Earth. If the United States were populated as densely as Bangladesh, it would contain the entire population of the planet.

Our population density is one of the reasons for our environmental vulnerability. The naturally rich resources of Bangladesh have been decimated in the desperate quest for economic growth to support our large population. Vast areas of the once-lush countryside have been deforested to produce wood and timber products for use in building homes, making furniture, and manufacturing paper and other goods. Rapidly growing industries without serious enforcement of environmental regulations have contributed to serious problems of water and air pollution. Reliance on wood- and charcoal-burning stoves for cooking and heat—even inside poorly ventilated homes—has led to thousands of cases of lung disease and related illnesses.

Some of these environmental problems can be addressed by technological and policy changes within Bangladesh itself. But even as Bangladesh works to tackle these challenges, a still bigger environmental problem over which Bangladesh has almost no influence is now threatening to obliterate vast portions of our country.

As a densely populated, low-lying country, with tens of millions of people living in or near the vast delta at the mouth of the Ganges River, Bangladesh has long been subject to devastating floods that periodically inundate large cities, wipe out countless farms and villages, and force millions of people to flee. These floods are one of the reasons for the country's persistent poverty. When farmers are repeatedly forced to start

from scratch after being wiped out every few years, it is difficult to amass the capital needed to build a more secure economic future.

Now our country is particularly vulnerable to the impacts of climate change. Environmental experts say that the
worldwide burning of fossil fuels and the heat-trapping gases
it produces are helping to melt the planet's ice caps, threatening a rise in sea levels of more than 3 feet by the end of the
twenty-first century. And although Bangladesh itself produces
just 0.3 percent of the global carbon emissions that are responsible for climate change, our country and its people will
be among the first victims. According to Atiq Rahman, executive director of the Bangladesh Centre for Advanced Studies
and a climate expert, by 2050 it's likely that rising seas will
permanently flood about 17 percent of Bangladesh, forcing
18 million people to flee.[1] And unless the world takes strong
steps to reverse the problem, that will just be the first stage of
the disaster.

For all these reasons, the people of Bangladesh join other
people in the world's poorest nations in being profoundly
committed to fixing the environmental practices that have
brought humankind to the brink of disaster. For simplicity, I
summarize this goal under the heading of *zero net carbon*. In
addition to eliminating all forms of environmental pollution,
our biggest goal should be to reduce emissions of climate-
altering carbon to the lowest possible levels—and to mitigate
the impact of the emissions we cannot eliminate through car-
bon-capturing practices such as tree planting. Since energy
consumption is a basic element in practically all economic activity, I find *zero net carbon* to be a convenient way to refer
to the entire range of environmental challenges that our new
economic framework must meet.

Some people in the wealthy nations of the world are surprised to learn how serious people in countries like Bangladesh, India, and China are about saving the health of our planet. They may assume that those of us in the developing nations who are eager to pursue economic growth would be relatively unconcerned about environmental problems. After all, this was the attitude of today's great economic powers during their own period of rapid growth. During the Industrial Revolution of the eighteenth and nineteenth centuries, and the continued expansion of mechanization and urbanization during the twentieth century, many countries in Europe and North America paid little heed to the environmental damage they were causing. Forests were razed, mountains of coal and oil were burned, diverse natural lands were turned over to monoculture, fishing stocks were depleted, and other resources were largely squandered.

Now people in the big industrial powers are trying, belatedly, to make up for the damage done. Perhaps it's understandable that they might assume that today's developing countries—nations like China, India, Brazil, Indonesia, and Vietnam—will follow the same path of heedless, reckless economic growth with no concern for environmental consequences. Some in the West who want to avoid committing effort and resources to environmental protection have even used this as an excuse for their own inaction. "We could spend billions of dollars on cleaning up our industries," they say. "But what's the point, when we know that China and India will never do the same? As the poorer nations of the world continue to develop, global pollution is bound to get worse no matter what we do in the West."

This is a false assumption, based on the mistaken belief that there is an inherent conflict between economic growth and environmental protection. In fact, it is quite possible to grow the economy, lifting communities and entire societies out of poverty, while also protecting the environment. Modern technologies make this easier to achieve than ever before. Scientists and engineers have made huge progress in developing renewable, sustainable sources of energy, less-polluting systems for manufacturing and shipping products, and techniques for agriculture, fishing, mining, and other forms of resource extraction that do not degrade the environment.

Thanks to these breakthroughs, today's developing nations are in many ways better positioned than the older industrialized nations to enjoy clean growth. They are not saddled with old legacy technologies—hundreds of power plants built to burn fossil fuels, wired communications grids that require resources to maintain, and old fleets of cars, trucks, and planes that waste fuel. This means they can leapfrog directly to more efficient, cleaner technologies that modern science has made available. There is no reason why we in the developing countries need to tolerate a period of rampant pollution and environmental destruction for the sake of economic growth. And, in fact, the biggest developing nations in the world, China and India, have joined the Paris Agreement that I discussed in Chapter 2 and are taking serious steps to carry out its provisions.

Unfortunately, the environmental record of Bangladesh is far from perfect. Today, even while the people of Bangladesh are appealing to the world to stop the environmental degradation that is hurting the country enormously, the government of Bangladesh is proceeding with two environmentally threatening projects.

One is a coal-fired, 1,320-megawatt power plant located at Rampal in the south of Bangladesh, very close to the Sundarbans, the world's largest mangrove forest. The project threatens the forest, which is a UNESCO World Heritage Site.

Public voices have been raised against this project, and convincing arguments have been presented by environmentalists from home and abroad. But the government is going ahead without paying attention to these voices of concern. Bangladesh needs power, but it should not be obtained at the cost of lives and livelihoods. By insisting on this project, Bangladesh is sending very wrong signals to the world—that internally it is not concerned with environmental issues, and that it seeks immediate economic gains at the cost of the environment. Those signals will reduce the support Bangladesh needs to overcome its accelerating problems being generated by global warming.

The second project is a nuclear power project designed to generate 2,000 megawatts of electricity. I've opposed nuclear power anywhere since the 1986 Chernobyl disaster, and my opposition was reconfirmed by the 2011 accident at the Japanese nuclear plants at Fukushima. Both of these events were loud wake-up calls. Each nuclear plant has the potential to cause massive, widespread devastation in terms of human life and misery over generations. Nuclear plants are vulnerable to natural disasters like earthquake and floods, as well as to human errors, negligence, and the risks of sabotage, terrorist attacks, and enemy assaults.

Bangladesh and the surrounding regions are the most densely populated in the world. I cannot imagine why we should plant something with the potential for mass destruction in the middle of the planet's most concentrated human population.

Bangladesh is an energy-starved country. Its economic growth, which has created the need for more energy, offers a good reason for Bangladesh to press the world to produce a global initiative to offer clean-energy solutions. These solutions exist. One of them requires collaboration among neighbors. The enormous capacity of Nepal to produce hydro power could easily be engaged for this purpose—a solution that would help put Bangladesh back on course to be a leader in the green environmental movement.

The international community of climate change activists could play a proactive role in addressing the energy problems of Bangladesh. These problems offer a great opportunity for this global community to express solidarity with this climate-challenged country by offering state-of-the-art technological options to generate green energy in a cost-effective way, along with help in funding such projects. As a result, Bangladesh would not feel forced into resorting to dirty energy, and a great example would be set for other countries facing the same problem. I believe there is still time for the world to come forward with these options so that Bangladesh will not choose the self-destructive paths of coal or nuclear power.

The fact is that there is no conflict among the three big goals I've set out for our new economic model. It is possible to pursue zero poverty and zero unemployment while also pursuing zero net carbon. In fact, it is essential to pursue all three goals, because they complement and support one another. If we chase economic growth in ways that destroy the environment, we will end up having to deal with trillions of dollars' worth of damage to our planet and to the resources on which all life ultimately depends. Dirty growth is unsustainable growth—not just in environmental terms but in practical economic terms as well.

Furthermore, history shows that when destructive environmental policies are pursued, the poor suffer most. Within the developed world, politicians, policy makers, and business leaders tend to make choices that put polluting, dangerous, toxic, and destructive industries and facilities in communities where poor people live. On a global scale, international companies find it cheap and easy to locate dirty industries in poor countries. When the people of a country are desperate for work and income, political leaders are tempted to ignore environmental problems and to eliminate or fail to enforce rules that would prevent polluting. The result may be jobs for the poor—but they are often dirty, dangerous, destructive jobs that leave poor communities worse off than before.

These environmental crimes committed against the poor are both a result of global inequality and a contributor to it, since rampant pollution makes it even harder for poor countries to lift themselves out of poverty. It's yet another example of how poor people suffer for problems that the entire human family contributes to. This pattern underscores why it is so essential to tackle all these problems together—because they all feed one another.

Grameen Shakti: Green Entrepreneurship Transforms the Energy Market

An example of how economic development and environmental protection can support one another rather than conflicting with one another can be seen in Grameen Shakti, the pioneering renewable energy business I launched in Bangladesh back in 1996.

When I wrote about Grameen Shakti in *Creating a World Without Poverty* (2007), the company had installed 100,000 solar panel systems in homes throughout Bangladesh. At the time, this achievement made Grameen Shakti one of the world's largest suppliers of solar home systems. Since then, renewable energy has grown at an amazing pace—and Grameen Shakti has led the way. We celebrated the installation of our one millionth solar home system with a ceremony in January 2013, and as of early 2017, the number of homes we serve has now surpassed 1.8 million.

It's difficult to overstate the importance of this accomplishment. Most villages in Bangladesh are not served by the national energy grid. Those that are connected find the energy supply often interrupted by outages. And, of course, traditional sources of electrical power like gas- or coal-fired plants contribute significantly to climate change, whose terrible impact on Bangladesh I've already mentioned.

For all these reasons, bringing clean, affordable, reliable energy to the homes of some 12 million Bangladeshis is a gigantic step forward. It provides schoolkids with electric lights by which they can do their homework. It enables shopkeepers, community centers, doctors' offices, and mosques to extend their hours into the evening, enriching countless lives and expanding economic opportunities. It helps farmers irrigate their lands and use labor-saving tools; it makes power-driven sewing machines available to rural female entrepreneurs. And it helps millions of Bangladeshis use the Internet to get access to the same sources of information and knowledge that people around the world rely on.

Just as the rural electrification program launched by the New Deal in the 1930s helped bring poverty-stricken areas of the American South into the twentieth-century economy, so the spread of solar energy is helping to integrate the villages of Bangladesh into the world of the twenty-first century.

Grameen Shakti isn't alone in making renewable energy available to the poor people of Bangladesh. Inspired by our success, some thirty additional companies—including both for-profit and nonprofit organizations—have sprung up to compete with Grameen Shakti, offering their own solar energy systems. We welcome this development, which has brought renewable electricity to an estimated 1.5 million more homes.

Grameen Shakti has diversified into other product offerings, all with the same focus on clean, renewable energy. Grameen Shakti sells an improved home cookstove that minimizes many of the problems with the traditional village stove design, reducing indoor pollution and fuel waste. About half a million of these improved stoves are now in use. Grameen Shakti has also installed tens of thousands of biogas plants, which convert natural wastes like cow dung into methane fuel for cooking.

Grameen Shakti has turned environmentally friendly technology into a successful social business and made it nationally replicable.

Haiti: Saving a Ravaged Countryside and the People Who Rely on It

In Chapter 4, I wrote at length about the importance of entrepreneurship as a driving force in reducing unemployment and combating poverty. As I explained, I believe traditional ideas of economic development have given far too much weight to the role of big corporations and giant industrial projects in generating economic growth. A healthier and more sustainable approach is to give equal if not greater weight to unleashing the creativity of millions of ordinary people who are perfectly capable of creating new business ideas that really meet the needs of the communities where they live. Giving such people the tools to convert their entrepreneurial dreams into realities—especially access to the investment capital they need to launch their companies—can help improve the economic outlooks of villages, cities, regions, and even entire countries.

But while I stress the importance of entrepreneurship as the bulwark of economic growth, I also recognize that big businesses have a role to play in creating the new economic system our world requires. Despite my academic training in economics, I am not a theorist or ideologue but rather a pragmatist—someone who has learned what works and what doesn't through trial and error, and through many real-world experiments. Over time, I've discovered that some social problems can benefit from the wise application of resources that big companies have in abundance, including money to spend, access to markets, sophisticated technology, and a large pool of talented people with management expertise and experience.

What is crucial, however, is that a big company that is interested in joining our new economic movement must be prepared to truly change its outlook—to leave behind the assumptions of the profit-maximization world and look at social challenges in a new light, with a new set of goals and metrics. This generally requires the presence of at least one visionary business leader at or near the top of the company—someone with the imagination to break free from old ways of thinking and the willingness to experiment with a new approach that calls on different aspects of human nature: idealism, generosity, unselfishness.

Four such business leaders that I've met in my work are Franck Riboud, chairman of Danone; Emmanuel Faber, CEO of Danone; Jean Bernou, regional president of McCain Foods; and Richard Branson, founder of the Virgin family of companies.

I've known Branson for several years. In addition to being a successful businessman and a flamboyant entrepreneur with a gift for colorful promotional stunts, Branson is also cofounder of an organization called the B Team. This is a group of business executives and other leaders who have taken on the challenge of "developing a 'Plan B'—for concerted, positive action that will ensure business becomes a driving force for social, environmental and economic benefit." The website for the organization goes on to say, "Plan A—where business has been motivated primarily by profit—is no longer an option."[2] The B Team is dedicated to pushing conventional businesses to move from their profit-only orientation toward a people-planet-profit orientation, giving all three goals equal status.

I am a member of the B Team. Among the others are the Internet entrepreneur Marc Benioff; media founder Arianna Huffington; Norwegian statesman and former director-general of the World Health Organization (WHO) Dr. Gro Harlem Brundtland; former president of Ireland Mary Robinson; Brazilian businessman Guilherme Leal; philanthropist Jochen Zeitz; and Kathy Calvin, president and CEO of the United Nations Foundation.

Knowing about Branson's interest in business projects that help people while protecting the planet, in 2013 I went to him with a project to invest in. Haiti Forest was designed by Yunus Social Business (YSB) as part of a big effort to reforest the island nation—a task that is crucial to lifting the people of Haiti out of the poverty in which too many of them are stuck.

Forests have always played a crucial role in the ecology and economy of Haiti. In the climate of the Caribbean, forests are essential to absorb the impact of tropical storms, help prevent soil erosion, and regulate the water cycle.

In 1923, 60 percent of Haiti was covered by forests. In the decades since then, however, these forests have been decimated. Several forces can be blamed. Big timber companies intensively logged large areas, wiping out centuries-old forests in just a few years. Logging set in motion a cycle that made it almost impossible for the forests to be rebuilt without outside intervention. Some of the companies tried to restock the forests by planting new trees, but these take many years to grow to full size. Local villagers, many of them desperately poor, cut down both mature trees and millions of young trees before they reached maturity, since they needed the wood to build shelters and to make charcoal, both as fuel for their fires and as a source of income.

Today, forests occupy just 2 percent of Haiti's land mass. The change has been devastating. In Haiti, as in other countries where forest lands have been destroyed, the vital carbon-trapping function of trees is greatly diminished, accelerating the destructive impact of climate change.

Agriculture is also powerfully affected. Without the forests, topsoil is easily removed by rainwater running down the mountainsides and ends up being deposited in rivers, lakes, and bays. Farmers are left with depleted, less-fertile soil, and water supplies are reduced because of accelerated runoff from the eroded earth. Poverty is more deeply entrenched than ever, and the cycle of forest destruction—and human suffering—continues unabated. The country's problems have been exacerbated by decades of authoritarian rule and by natural disasters such as the devastating earthquake that hit Haiti in 2010. These environmental troubles are one of the reasons that Haiti is the poorest country in the Western Hemisphere.

Haiti Forest has been launched to start the process of reforesting Haiti piece by piece. It is a social business initiative supported by nongovernmental organizations like the Nature Conservancy, which is providing environmental, agricultural, and forestry expertise. In addition, Branson's Virgin Unite charitable foundation and the Clinton Foundation are providing a combination of philanthropic gifts and social business investments, where the initial funding will be repaid without interest or dividends. Haiti Forest aims to plant over a million trees each year, with the goal of reforesting 1,000 hectares (almost 2,500 acres) around the town of Saint-Michel-de-l'Attalaye in the Central Plateau region of Haiti.

In addition to improving the severely damaged natural habitat of Haiti, the project will improve the livelihoods of farmers. Production of forest-based goods such as fruit, coffee, and oils is being expanded, bringing increased revenues to farmers and employment to local people. The project will also create additional jobs outside the farming sector by helping to support entrepreneurial businesses that market goods made from forest-grown materials.

One example is Kreyol Essence, an eco-luxury beauty brand based on products made from Haitian black castor oil. The company was founded by Yve-Car Momperousse and Stéphane Jean-Baptiste, two Haitian Americans who were living in Philadelphia when Yve-Car suffered a "hair catastrophe"—her hair was damaged by a hairdresser applying too much heat during a treatment. Yve-Car recalled that women in her native Haiti used local black castor oil as a remedy for damaged hair, and she sought out the product in America—with no success. She and Stéphane were inspired to start a business that would revive this old tradition and make it available to women around the world.

Today, Kreyol Essence works together with Haitian farmers, mainly female. The company plants castor trees in cooperation with these female smallholder farmers, and afterward buys the castor plants and the oil-producing castor seeds at above-market price to ensure sustainable incomes for those in the castor oil value chain. It is one of a number of entrepreneurial businesses that is helping to advance the goal of reforesting the devastated countryside of Haiti, while at the same time creating economic activity that helps to alleviate the rampant poverty from which Haitians suffer.

Uganda: Entrepreneurial Solutions to Everyday Environmental Challenges

In Chapter 2, I wrote about how the economic prospects of the African country of Uganda have been enhanced by a rising tide of entrepreneurship. Young Ugandans have started businesses, generating economic activity and creating the possibility for their homeland to take a step forward out of poverty.

Because Uganda is still a poor country, with almost one quarter of its people living below the official poverty line, the quest for economic growth is important. But economic growth must not be pursued at the price of environmental sustainability. Like Haiti, and like many other countries in the developing world, Uganda has significant ecological problems that demand attention. A growing population has led to uncontrolled agricultural expansion, damaging essential forest reserves and wetlands and causing soil erosion and reduction of water supplies. Today some 20 percent of Ugandan city dwellers and over 50 percent of rural villagers lack access to pure drinking water. Pollution generated by the growing population and by poorly regulated manufacturing and mining industries has introduced toxins into the water supply. Pollution also threatens a number of rare bird, animal, and plant species, which are precious in themselves and serve as important attractions for visitors to the country's national parks and wildlife refuges.

Given the urgency of these environmental challenges, it's important for the social business entrepreneurs of Uganda not just to create jobs and support economic growth but also to tackle problems like pollution and water quality, so that the lives of the people of Uganda can be enhanced in every way—not merely in terms of dollars and cents. YSB Uganda's program basket contains a number of entrepreneurial social businesses that have placed environmental problems at the heart of their mission.

One of these social businesses is Savco Millers, which makes and sells products using recycled plastic wastes. Like many fast-growing cities around the world, Kampala, the capital of Uganda, has a huge problem dealing with an ever-expanding flood of trash, much of it plastic—grocery bags, product packages, water and soda bottles, and the like. It is estimated that over 108 tons of plastic waste are generated in Uganda every day, yet the recycling capacity is less than half that amount. Much of this trash ends up in urban dumps that are unsightly and unhealthy, blighting the neighborhoods where the poor people of Kampala live.

However, the steady accumulation of plastic waste also creates a business opportunity for the entrepreneurial-minded residents of Kampala. Many of them supplement their incomes by sorting through the garbage in local dumps, picking out scraps of plastic that can be recycled and sold. It's dirty, dangerous work, but at least it generates some badly needed income for poor people.

The mission of Savco Millers, a social business supported by YSB, is to improve this work for the people of Kampala while also reducing the environmental problems caused by the plastic blight. The company works directly with plastic collectors, providing them with training, protective equipment, and an unusually high fixed price for the plastic they gather. The premium price is made possible by the fact that Savco cuts out the intermediaries who normally handle the collection process—and claim an exorbitant share of the proceeds. Savco Millers then processes the plastic in its own plant, converting it into new products like grow bags for trees, construction sheets, and waste collection bags. The products are sold back to the local community at affordable prices.

Some of the collectors who work with Savco Millers have been able to escape from homelessness and poverty as a result—for example, William Male, a former "street kid" in Kampala who credits his plastic waste collecting business with saving him from a life centered on "pickpocketing and sniffing glue." So Savco Millers is using its simple yet powerful business model to simultaneously address two pressing social issues—unemployment and environmental degradation.

Another social business supported by YSB is Green Bio Energy, a company based in Bugolobi, a neighborhood of Kampala some 4½ miles south of the city's bustling center. Green Bio Energy makes and markets two main lines of products: charcoal briquettes used in household and commercial cooking, and small, portable cookstoves, each large enough to hold and heat a single pot.

Both charcoal and charcoal-burning cookstoves are familiar to everyone in Uganda. The charcoal is usually made by cutting down trees from Uganda's rapidly shrinking forests and burning them. But the versions of these products offered by Green Bio Energy are different from others. Both have been engineered, designed, and manufactured to be environmentally and economically friendly. The charcoal briquettes, sold in big paper bags under the Briketi brand name, are made completely from recycled charcoal and various forms of agricultural waste—cassava and banana peelings, rice husks, coffee pulp, and so on. This dramatically reduces the need to cut down trees. They are also long-burning, which makes them more economical for the families that use them, and clean-burning—that is, they produce much less soot and smoke than traditional charcoal. This is an important benefit for women who often spend hours bending over a stove inside small, poorly ventilated homes.

Best of all, the briquettes are retailed at just around US$2 for a 5-kilogram bag. This is enough to serve the typical family for five days. It's a reasonable price that even most poor families can afford. No wonder the Briketi briquettes are now the best sellers in the Kampala market, popular not only among families but also with business customers—restaurants, hospitals, schools, and anyone else who does cooking.

Meanwhile, the Briketi brand EcoStove embodies a series of small but significant improvements on the traditional design of the Ugandan home cookstove. These include smaller and more numerous air vents, more consistent thickness of ceramic surfaces, and a low center of gravity. These design modifications make the stove highly energy-efficient, clean-burning, and safe to use, with reduced risk of spilling or tipping over. The stoves are sold in urban grocery stores and in little shops and kiosks in the villages, and they've proven to be enormously popular. In the first three years after EcoStove was launched in 2013, sales soared from about 80 units per month to over 2,500.

Founded in 2011 by a couple of French expats who'd fallen in love with Uganda and its people, Green Bio Energy now employs more than seventy local people in managerial, sales, logistics, and production roles. The company's engineering team and its research and development staff are working on more new product ideas, all dedicated to environmentally friendly solutions for Uganda.

One more example of a social business with an environmental mission supported by YSB is Impact Water. I've mentioned that water pollution is a big problem in Uganda. Over 9 million Ugandans lack access to safe drinking water, and an estimated 440 children die every week of waterborne diseases. A much higher number fall sick and experience health issues from contaminated water, which results in lower school attendance. This is a great example of how poverty, unemployment, and environmental degradation are interrelated problems. Poor people are those most likely to lack potable water; poor children get sick from waterborne diseases and miss school; as a result, many fall behind in their classes and fail to graduate altogether. This greatly increases their chances of suffering unemployment and falling even deeper into poverty . . . and so the cycle continues.

Millions of Ugandans try to solve this problem by boiling water before using it. It's a costly, time-consuming process that demands great patience; many people don't bother to boil the water sufficiently and end up with drinking water in which contaminants linger. And because wood is the most popular fuel for fires, the need to boil water daily contributes to the deforestation problem I've already mentioned.

Impact Water seeks to break this cycle by making safe drinking water available where children spend most of their time—at schools. Company engineers have developed a variety of water purification systems designed to produce great results at the lowest possible cost, geared to the needs of schools of differing sizes and with varied water sources. For small schools, a ceramic filtration system that delivers 3 to 5 liters of water per hour with no need for electricity is sufficient. For larger schools, an ultrafiltration system that streams water through carbon filters and hollow-fiber membranes, again without need for electricity, is appropriate. And for the largest schools, an ultraviolet disinfection system that purifies water for storage in a big stainless steel tank is recommended. The latter system requires just one to two hours' access to electricity per day—a reasonable requirement in a country where the power grid is unreliable and, in some areas, inaccessible.

Impact Water enhances its offerings to schools by providing two years' worth of preventive maintenance (included with every installation) and well-designed payment systems that make pure water affordable even to small schools with access to modest funds. For example, Impact Water works with schools to time their installment payments to match up with the receipt of school fees. The company has signed up schools across the country by marketing clean drinking water as an attractive amenity to be offered to families. Schools with Impact Water filtration systems can present themselves proudly as modern schools that promote the well-being of their students—who are likely to remain healthy and therefore miss fewer classes as a result.

As of late 2016, Impact Water has already installed its systems in more than a thousand schools with a combined student population of over half a million. Even as the company seeks to attract more school customers, it is also working on plans to expand into new markets, such as military barracks and prisons. The more effectively Impact Water can reach large numbers of people with its institutionally based water solutions, the bigger the effect it can have on the problem of waterborne diseases.

Uganda is a rapidly growing country with a variety of environmental problems in need of solutions. Entrepreneurial social businesses like Savco Millers, Green Bio Energy, and Impact Water are tackling these problems from the ground up while also fueling employment and continued economic growth. They are helping to prove that traditional assumptions about the link between economic development and environmental degradation are no longer valid, and that clean growth is not a fantasy but a reality.

The New Economy and the Goal of Zero Net Carbon

As the examples I've discussed illustrate, a growing number of social businesses around the world are dedicated specifically to selling goods and services that address environmental problems, from deforestation to mountains of plastic trash to lack of potable water. But one basic principle is that all social businesses must be environmentally sustainable—no matter whether their main purpose is to reduce poverty, to provide health care, to improve education, or anything else.

I hope the reason is obvious: the goal of our economic experimentation is to make the world a better place. If a social business helps reduce unemployment or enhances child nutrition, but at the same time it helps to destroy the environment and render our planet less able to sustain life, then no long-term benefit for humankind has really been created. Humans are absolutely reliant on a healthy planet for our very existence. So it's impossible to imagine a true social business that does not treat the environment with the respect and care it deserves.

It would be a mistake, however, to think that social business alone can solve the environmental crises we face. We need to address the issues from all sides, including concerns about lifestyle; government policies about energy, mining, and businesses; and other factors. And since profit-maximizing businesses will represent the great bulk of business activity for the foreseeable future, we must insist that they operate in an environmentally responsible fashion. Government regulations as well as social pressure from customers and citizens' groups will play an important part in enforcing this norm. It would make no sense to create a world in which social businesses are working to repair the damage to the environment that human behavior has caused while at the same time profit-maximizing companies are allowed to create fresh damage.

This means that companies of all kinds are required to join this giant initiative to simply uphold our shared humanity, to behave in an ethical, responsible fashion toward the environment that we all depend upon. What is unique about social businesses is that, because they have no incentive to pursue profit, they have greater flexibility and freedom to experiment with new ways to improve and repair the environment. Freedom from market expectations and the demand for ever-growing profits permits social businesses to advance goals like protecting the global commons—our universal heritage of clean air, water, farmland, and other resources—without worrying about whether their activities can be used to enrich individuals.

The need for social businesses that address environmental issues is just as pressing in the developed nations as it is in low-income countries like Haiti and Uganda. It's easy to imagine social businesses in the wealthy countries of North America, Europe, and East Asia dedicated to meeting needs that range from renewable energy to trash recycling, safe drinking water to sustainable farming practices, less-wasteful product packaging to energy-efficient transportation systems. The possibilities are limited only by the human imagination.

Advancing toward the goal of zero net carbon is a giant task that requires contributions from all people and all kinds of organizations. A new economic framework that makes ample room for businesses dedicated to social goals is an essential prerequisite to achieving that goal.

6

A ROAD MAP TO A
BETTER FUTURE

Public attitudes about the world and its future seem to swing wildly from one extreme to another, often connected with political waves or with the presence or absence of inspiring global leaders at a given time. Sometimes, the news media and the general public appear to be very optimistic and hopeful; other times, they sink into pessimism and even despair.

Right now, we seem to be experiencing a period of extreme pessimism. Many people appear to be cynical about the idea that anything can be done to fix the world's most serious problems; they speak as if national governments, nonprofit organizations, and international agencies are powerless to produce any meaningful change. Some seem to have concluded that human beings are unable to do anything to interfere with the outcomes produced by the "free market," which is presumed to be all-powerful.

As I've made clear in this book, I consider the problems humankind currently faces to be very serious. Issues like wealth concentration, global poverty, disparities in health care and education, disregard of human rights, environmental degradation, and climate change are all in need of immediate, concerted attention. In a few cases—particularly in regard to climate change—expert opinion suggests we may be near a crucial turning point that demands strong, quick actions to avoid potentially catastrophic events.

However, although I regard the problems faced by human society as quite serious, I am fundamentally optimistic about the future. I am convinced that we have it within our power to make all the changes needed to solve these problems and to make life fundamentally better for practically everyone on Earth.

There are a number of reasons for my optimism. One of the most fundamental reasons is simple logic: since the problems we face are made by humans, they can be solved by humans. Changing our thinking and our behavior will have a dramatic impact on the future of our civilization.

Another reason I am optimistic is the fact that there are already hopeful stories of international cooperation and success. One of these is the story of the Millennium Development Goals and the Sustainable Development Goals.

The Millennium Development Goals (MDGs) were established following the Millennium Summit of the United Nations in 2000. All 189 United Nations member states at that time, and at least 22 international organizations, committed to help the world achieve the eight MDGs by 2015. The goals were:

1. To eradicate extreme poverty and hunger
2. To achieve universal primary education
3. To promote gender equality and empower women
4. To reduce child mortality

5. To improve maternal health
6. To combat HIV/AIDS, malaria, and other diseases
7. To ensure environmental sustainability
8. To develop a global partnership for development

EACH GOAL HAD SPECIFIC TARGETS and dates for achieving those targets. To accelerate progress, the finance ministers of the world's eight leading economic powers (known as the G8), decided in June 2005 to put some additional financial clout behind their commitments. They agreed to provide enough funds to development banks and to the International Monetary Fund (IMF) to cancel US$40 billion to US$55 billion in debt owed by some of the poorest nations in the world, which would allow those countries to redirect resources to programs for reducing poverty and for improving health and education.

The very existence of the MDGs represented a milestone in human history. Before they were crafted, there was no framework for promoting global progress agreed upon by leaders of the nations of the world, including both the wealthy nations and the poorer nations. The agreement on the MDGs was the most important set of decisions ever made on the basis of global consensus with quantifiable goals.

As you might expect, the MDGs were greeted with enthusiasm by optimists like me, while pessimists and cynics shrugged their shoulders, expecting little or nothing positive to happen. Now the deadline for the ambitious goals of the MDGs has passed. What have the results been, and what have we learned from the experience?

Optimists like me are celebrating the world's accomplishments through the MDGs, while pessimists are pointing out the failures of the MDGs. I am happy about the recognition that Bangladesh has received from its great successes, particularly its success in reducing poverty. Bangladesh's national goal was to reduce the poverty rate to 29 percent by the year 2015. Two years ahead of time, in 2013, the poverty rate was reduced to 26.2 percent, almost three percentage points better than the goal. Bangladesh has also achieved full gender parity in primary and secondary enrollment, a sharp reduction in infant and child mortality, and major improvement in maternal health care. In the end, Bangladesh made significant progress on all of the eight MDGs. That is quite a list of accomplishments, one that has done a lot to boost the morale of the people of Bangladesh and prepared them to do still better in the future.

When measured against the eight goals, the progress achieved by the countries of the world was uneven. A number of countries achieved several of the goals, while others, plagued by problems such as political dysfunction and financial shortfalls, achieved none. It's important to remember that the last seven years of the MDG program—practically half of the entire process—took place in the shadow of the Great Recession, the worst economic collapse since the Great Depression of the 1930s, whose impact on the developing world was even greater than on the wealthy nations of the West.

And yet, against this backdrop, it's remarkable to recognize the extraordinary progress that was actually accomplished in regard to all of the global MDG targets. Although the world as a whole did not achieve the goals, individual countries, like Bangladesh, reached some of the toughest goals while doing remarkably well in others. A number of significant global accomplishments were also achieved. Here are some examples:

- The world succeeded in reducing the number of people living in extreme poverty (defined as an income of less than US$1.25 per day) by more than half—from 1.9 billion people in 1990 to 836 million in 2015.

- While the goal of universal primary education was not met, the school enrollment rate in the developing nations reached 91 percent by 2015—a big improvement over previous years, and a huge step toward the goal of 100 percent participation.
- Many measures of gender equality improved significantly. For example, whereas in 1990 only 74 girls in South Asia were enrolled in school for every 100 boys, by 2015, 103 girls were enrolled for every 100 boys. The share of women in national legislatures nearly doubled between 1990 and 2015 (though women still make up only about 20 percent of the world's lawmakers).
- The rate of child mortality fell by more than half, from 90 per 1,000 in 1990 to 43 per 1,000 in 2015.
- New HIV infections fell by around 40 percent between 2000 and 2013, while the incidence of malaria fell by around 37 percent, saving an estimated 6.2 million lives.

WE LIVE IN AN AGE unlike any other in history—an age when society has enormous economic resources, unprecedented technological tools, and relatively higher levels of peace, freedom, and cooperation than humans have ever experienced. As the impressive progress achieved through the MDGs suggests, human society can accomplish whatever goals we are honestly determined to achieve. That is the most important reason I am one of the optimists about the future of our species, and why I am eager to enlist more allies in the battle to accomplish even greater feats in the years ahead.

A GLOBAL TO-DO LIST—THE SUSTAINABLE DEVELOPMENT GOALS

BUOYED BY THE ENCOURAGING RESULTS of the MDG process, the nations of the UN have now gotten together to create an even more ambitious set of global goals. These are the Sustainable Development Goals (SDGs). Developed through an extensive process of study, consultation, and discussion that involved technical experts, policy makers, and social activists from countries all over the word, the SDGs include seventeen overarching goals and 169 specific targets, each defined in quantifiable terms so that progress can be clearly defined, monitored, and measured. The broad objective is to achieve all seventeen goals by the year 2030.

Like the MDGs, the SDGs represent a remarkable breakthrough in the history of human civilization. Never before have representatives of the entire planet joined forces to address the problems facing the whole human species—rich and poor, male and female, young and old, of every race, culture, and creed—by pursuing an ambitious set of shared goals crafted within a framework that reflects the environmental realities that will shape the future of life on Earth.

The word *sustainable* in the title of the SDGs is the most significant message of the goals. Everything we do, from building infrastructure and creating new industries to founding cities and developing innovative technologies, affects all of us as well as the planetary ecosystem on which we rely. The ways we choose to employ natural resources, address changing human demographics, produce and consume energy, and share the wealth produced through social activities—all these actions have an impact on the natural environment and therefore on the future viability of our species. We need to start making these decisions not based on immediate or short-term needs but with the hopes and needs of future generations in mind.

This is what *sustainability* means. It means eating the fruits without harming the trees, and in fact making the trees more productive along the way so that over time everybody will be able to enjoy more fruit. Over the past few decades, government officials, scientists, economists, businesspeople, social activists, and other leaders have all gradually come together around the recognition that any plan or program for future development must be designed with sustainability in mind.

The clearest example of how our thinking must change to embrace the demands of sustainability is the problem of climate change. Thirty to forty years ago, when a few far-seeing experts on Earth's biosphere were beginning to warn us about the danger posed by carbon emissions, most people thought they were crazy. "The world has gone on for millions of years with continual changes in climate and weather, and now you are saying that the pollution from a few cars and factories is going to doom our planet in the next fifty or seventy years? You are out of your mind."

Almost no one talks that way any longer. As the scientific evidence piles up, we now understand how climatic changes in the distant past actually led to numerous instances of catastrophic species extinctions, including the demise of the dinosaurs some 65 million years ago. We are also seeing clear signs of how today's global climate is evolving, and doing so far more rapidly than the experts ever imagined. Finally, government leaders have gotten together and said, "We have to stop this here. We must take steps to prevent the average global temperature from rising more than 1.5 degrees Celsius above its level before the start of the industrial era." The Paris Agreement, which I wrote about in Chapter 2, was the result. It lays out basic practices and principles that must be followed to ensure that the economic activities we undertake in the years to come will no longer contribute to the problem of global warming.

But climate change is not the only sustainability problem the human species faces. Other changes affecting the relationship between humans and the natural environment must also be examined with our long-term survival in mind. For example, even apart from the impact on global climate, we can't continue to exist as a species if we continue to cut down the world's forests at the current rate. We can't hope to meet the future nutritional needs of the human population if we continue to harvest the world's fish and other ocean life as we are now doing. The ability of tomorrow's farmers to feed the people of the world will be compromised if we continue to practice chemical-based monocultures that deplete the soil and increase the vulnerability of crops to blights and diseases. Continued overuse of antibiotics enhances the risk of devastating epidemics that could kill hundreds of millions of people. Unless we learn to stop letting plastic waste find its way into our canals and rivers, where it ends up contributing to the growing plastic patch in the middle of the Pacific Ocean, we'll soon be eating fish laced with indigestible plastic microgranules and drinking water containing microfibers of plastic.

All of these are examples of how the decisions we make today help to determine how sustainable life on this planet will be in the decades and centuries to come.

Furthermore, sustainability also involves social, economic, and political challenges that are not directly related to environmental or biological factors. Take the problem of economic inequality. If current trends continue, with more and more wealth and income being channeled to an ever-smaller fraction of the population, stresses and tensions among social groups will inevitably become worse. Desperately poor people will be driven to crime; civil unrest, riots, and violence will break out among people who have been forced into slums or camps by the dysfunctional economic system; refugees by the millions will flood across national borders, demanding a fair share of the resources that the richest nations have accumulated; and wars between countries over economic resources, from oil and minerals to water and farmland, will become increasingly likely. Democratic societies torn by economic strife will be tempted to give power to oligarchs who promise to control civic unrest by building walls and arming militias to keep the poor in their place.

Human society will not be sustainable under those circumstances. In practical terms, economic fairness is inextricably linked to our hopes for a just, democratic, and peaceful society.

Overcoming poverty is an essential aspect of ensuring peace among people. Fair distribution of wealth is ultimately a sustainability issue, just as much as climate change, air pollution, or overuse of natural resources.

The seventeen goals that constitute the SDGs must be read with these realities in mind. Together, they present a compelling vision for a better world that we can build—or at least put well on the way to being built—by the target date of 2030.

The seventeen Sustainable Development Goals are as follows:

1. No Poverty: End poverty in all its forms everywhere.
2. Zero Hunger: End hunger, achieve food security and improved nutrition, and promote sustainable agriculture.
3. Good Health and Well-being: Ensure healthy lives and promote well-being for all at all ages.

4. Quality Education: Ensure inclusive and equitable quality education and promote lifelong learning opportunities for all.

5. Gender Equality: Achieve gender equality and empower all women and girls.

6. Clean Water and Sanitation: Ensure availability and sustainable management of water and sanitation for all.

7. Affordable and Clean Energy: Ensure access to affordable, reliable, sustainable, and modern energy for all.

8. Decent Work and Economic Growth: Promote sustained, inclusive, and sustainable economic growth; full and productive employment; and decent work for all.

9. Industry, Innovation, and Infrastructure: Build resilient infrastructure, promote inclusive and sustainable industrialization, and foster innovation.

10. Reduced Inequalities: Reduce income inequality within and among countries.

11. Sustainable Cities and Communities: Make cities and human settlements inclusive, safe, resilient, and sustainable.

12. Responsible Consumption and Production: Ensure sustainable consumption and production patterns.

13. Climate Action: Take urgent action to combat climate change and its impacts by regulating emissions and promoting developments in renewable energy.

14. Life Below Water: Conserve and sustainably use the oceans, seas, and marine resources for sustainable development.

15. Life on Land: Protect, restore, and promote sustainable use of terrestrial ecosystems, sustainably manage forests, combat desertification, and halt and reverse land degradation and halt biodiversity loss.

16. Peace, Justice, and Strong Institutions: Promote peaceful and inclusive societies for sustainable development, provide access to justice for all, and build effective, accountable and inclusive institutions at all levels.

17. Partnerships for the Goals: Strengthen the means of implementation and revitalize the global partnership for sustainable development.[1]

Each of the seventeen goals is associated with a number of specific targets. For example, under the heading of goal 1, No Poverty, the UN has established the following seven targets:

- By 2030, eradicate extreme poverty for all people everywhere, currently measured as people living on less than US$1.25 a day.
- By 2030, reduce at least by half the proportion of men, women, and children of all ages living in poverty in all its dimensions according to national definitions.
- Implement nationally appropriate social protection systems and measures for all, including floors [i.e. minimum standards], and by 2030 achieve substantial coverage of the poor and the vulnerable.
- By 2030, ensure that all men and women, in particular the poor and the vulnerable, have equal rights

to economic resources, as well as access to basic services, ownership and control over land and other
forms of property, inheritance, natural resources,
appropriate new technology, and financial services,
including microfinance.

- By 2030, build the resilience of the poor and those in
  vulnerable situations and reduce their exposure and
  vulnerability to climate-related extreme events and
  other economic, social and environmental shocks
  and disasters.

- Ensure significant mobilization of resources from a
  variety of sources, including through enhanced development cooperation, in order to provide adequate
  and predictable means for developing countries,
  in particular least developed countries, to implement programs and policies to end poverty in all its
  dimensions.

- Create sound policy frameworks at the national, regional, and international levels, based on pro-poor
  and gender-sensitive development strategies, to support accelerated investment in poverty eradication
  actions.[2]

YOU'LL NOTICE THAT THESE TARGETS are defined as clearly
and specifically as possible, including quantitative objectives
wherever appropriate, so that expert analysts and social advocates can draw objective conclusions as to whether the targets
have been met and, if not, exactly how and where the shortfalls have occurred so that remedial steps can be undertaken.
The successes already achieved under the MDGs give us good
reasons to hope for even more accomplishments under the
auspices of the SDGs. For example, the fact that Bangladesh

reduced its poverty rate by half between 2000 and 2013 makes it plausible to imagine that we can eliminate extreme poverty altogether by 2030.

As with the Millennium Development Goals, countries, for-profit companies, nonprofit organizations, and influential individuals around the world have been signing up to support the SDGs. The great powers of the world—countries like the United States and China, all of the world's major financial institutions, giant global corporations, and of course the United Nations itself—will need to play major roles in promoting achievement of all seventeen goals. And countless people and groups are already engaged in activities and advocacy to support the SDGs. No matter what kind of work you do or what your main interests are as a concerned citizen and a social activist, you can find one or more of the SDGs that you can directly support in your community and in the world.

I'm honored to be one of the individuals involved in spreading awareness of and commitment to the SDGs around the world. In January 2016, UN Secretary-General Ban-Ki Moon announced the formation of a group of advocates dedicated to promoting the SDGs. With a mandate to support the secretary-general in his efforts to generate momentum and commitment to achieve the SDGs by 2030, the SDG Advocates have added their voices to spur action on the visionary and transformational sustainable development agenda. They are engaging with partners from civil society, academia, national legislatures on every continent, and leaders from the private sector to develop new and groundbreaking ideas and ways to promote SDG implementation.

As an SDG Advocate, I'm encouraging everybody to adopt the SDGs as their personal goals, and as goals for any organization, business, or civic association they are associated with, belong to, or have influence on. As citizens of the world, we have to do all we can to make sure we succeed in implementing every one of them.

The unfortunate truth is that our current world civilization is not sustainable, for environmental, social, and economic reasons. To guarantee our future, we need to create a new civilization—a task that we cannot walk away from. The SDGs provide a powerful agenda for the kinds of changes we must bring about. The fact that the nations of the world have agreed to jointly shoulder this task is a remarkable step in human history.

How New-Economy Businesses Will Drive Achievement of the SDGs

An old road always leads to an old destination. If we want to reach a new destination very different from the old one, we have to build a new road. There are no exceptions to this rule.

Social business will play a central role in creating a new road toward the new civilization we need. This makes sense in theory, and practical experience bears it out. Many social businesses are already helping the implementation of one or more of the SDGs.

One of the geographic areas in which Yunus Social Business (YSB) has been active is the Balkans—the poorest part of the European continent and a region in which unemployment, poverty, environmental degradation, and declining social institutions have all been major problems for a long time.

Long dominated by the Soviet Union, the countries of the Balkan Peninsula in southeastern Europe economically lagged behind the rest of the continent. With the collapse of the Soviet Union and the end of the Cold War, the Balkans began a transition to free-market economies. But this transition was disrupted by internal wars that followed the breakup of the multiethnic nation of Yugoslavia. Beginning in 1991, a series of independent nations gradually emerged, including Slovenia, Croatia, Bosnia and Herzegovina, Macedonia, Montenegro, and Serbia. The longstanding conflicts among ethnic groups, along with humanitarian crimes committed by leaders such as the Serbian dictator Slobodan Milosevic, caused enormous suffering in the region and crippled economic and social development. Millions of people were displaced from their homes; many thousands fled the region as refugees.

Today, most of the Balkan countries are at peace. But the peoples of the region continue to struggle economically. Per capita GDP in Albania, Serbia, and the other countries of the Western Balkans is about one quarter that of countries in Western Europe such as Germany, France, and the United Kingdom. Years of neglect, underinvestment, and destruction in warfare have left the region with inadequate infrastructure and badly damaged social and economic structures. Despite efforts to promote physical, economic, and social reconstruction, the unemployment rate in Bosnia and Herzegovina, for example, is a shockingly high 40 percent (2017).

Members of the YSB team began their work in the Balkans by studying economic and social conditions and talking with local people from many walks of life. They were looking for an opening where social business concepts can be applied and can make a small beginning. They met a large number of aspiring entrepreneurs—many of them very well educated—who were eager to use their creativity and talents to bring new life to their homelands but were crippled by a lack of investment capital and other structural challenges. For example, 85 percent of the entrepreneurs interviewed by YSB staff stated that interest rates from conventional banks are too high to support startup businesses. This forces three quarters of them to rely on informal sources—family and friends, for example—to scrape together the money needed to launch a company. Complicated taxation and regulation challenges complicate the startup process as well.[3]

In response, YSB developed an accelerator program for Balkan entrepreneurs similar to those provided by venture capitalists for promising high-tech businesses in Silicon Valley and elsewhere, but from a different context: the context of social business. In one typical weeklong workshop held in Tirana, the capital of Albania, budding entrepreneurs were given a good understanding of social business and were trained in skills like market analysis, customer development, and product design and testing in the context of designing a social business.

The training YSB provides is focused on applying the new business concept of social business to address social problems specific to the challenges faced by the people in the country and the problems faced by entrepreneurs. For example, one of the main challenges many entrepreneurs seek to address is the difficulty of accessing wealthy markets in the big cities of Europe through export programs, wholesaler networks, or large retail chains. The YSB team includes experts who can help find ways to overcome these barriers.

One of the companies that benefited from YSB's support is Udruzene, a Bosnia-based company that produces world-class handicraft products through knitting and crocheting.

Udruzene's founder, Nadira Mingasson, fled her native Bosnia at age nineteen when war broke out. She ended up in Paris, where she became part of the city's world-famous fashion industry. In 2008, on a visit home, she discovered the beautiful handmade fabrics made by poor rural women and realized that this represented a creative and business opportunity. She launched Udruzene, which means "unified women" in the Bosnian language.

Today, garments made by Udruzene's craftswomen are marketed by some of the most prominent fashion designers in Germany, Japan, Norway, Italy, and other countries. "I knew that the women could meet those standards," Mingasson says. "They only needed to update their skills."[4] The products are created by women in rural areas of the Balkans—skilled artisans who otherwise would almost surely be victimized by the rampant unemployment in their homelands. Udruzene currently employs more than three hundred knitters from around Bosnia and Herzegovina—each of them an entrepreneur in her own right, enabled to reach a broader marketplace through the sales and distribution channels provided by Udruzene. In this way, Udruzene helps women who have suffered from war, violence, and social marginalization, using knitting as a way to help reintegrate them into society through economic and social empowerment by creating a social business.

Another Balkan social business company supported by YSB that is creating business opportunities for individual entrepreneurs throughout the region is Rizona, which has created a reliable market for high-quality, organically farmed processed vegetables produced by one hundred small farmers in the Rahovec region of Kosovo. A third is St. George Valley Organic Farm, a medical herbs social business company founded by a local man named Emiland Skora. Located close to Tirana, St. George plants herbs that can be distilled into herbal essences, which in turn are sold on the international markets for use in medical applications or cosmetic purposes—a much higher-margin business than most forms of agriculture. St. George rents the land to some sixty local farmers and educates them about the techniques and practices of herbal farming, enabling them to create more income for themselves and their families. And because the medicinal use of the herbs requires strictly organic processes, this business is environmentally friendly as well.

As these examples show, a social business is a problem-solving business. No matter which problem a social business focuses on, it is directly and indirectly addressing some of the SDGs, creating income opportunities, jobs, gender equality, poverty reduction, and so on.

Two further examples of social business I'll present here are from Colombia and France. They are interesting on several counts. Both are joint ventures with a mega company involved in agriculture, particularly food production.

Campo Vivo, a business venture in the Latin American nation of Colombia, was created by YSB in partnership with McCain Foods, a family-owned Canada-based company that was founded in 1957 and has been well established in Europe and around the world since the 1960s.

Jean Bernou, McCain's regional president for continental Europe, the Middle East, and North Africa, is an unusual person. Based in Lille, France, Bernou became very interested in the idea of social business several years ago. He started attending conferences and meetings wherever I was speaking, and began calling me to discuss ways in which McCain's business resources, talent, and expertise could contribute to developing a new economic system for addressing the world's most challenging problems. He also introduced me and some other members of the Grameen team to members of the founding

McCain family in Canada. They, too, became interested in the social business concept and wanted to get involved with it. The opportunity for us to work together ultimately emerged when YSB started looking for solutions for some of the economic problems afflicting the poorest people in Colombia.

Approximately 31 percent of Colombia's population live in rural areas, where poor communities generally rely on farming as the main source of income. Rural farmers in Colombia often face severe challenges, just like everywhere else, including restricted access to capital, new farming technologies, and technical assistance, as well as weak bargaining power for the sale of their crops. In recent years, these economic problems have become particularly acute. Colombia has lost much of its market for the once-famous Colombian coffee. When Asian producers in countries like Vietnam and Indonesia took over increasing shares of the coffee market, Colombian coffee farmers suddenly faced a serious economic crisis, one that plunged entire communities into near-depression conditions.

McCain specializes in growing, processing, and marketing potatoes. In fact, every year, McCain processes over 5 million tons of potatoes into French fries and related products in its factories around the world. With the popularity of American-style French fries continuing to grow, we recognized an opportunity for the suffering Colombian farmers to switch to a new line of business. That's how the idea for Campo Vivo was born.

Campo Vivo is a joint venture between McCain Foods and YSB with the mission to improve the livelihoods of local farmers and their families living in disadvantaged communities in rural Colombia that lack sufficient access to markets and networks to sell their products. The company applies McCain's unmatched potato expertise by helping Colombian

farmers grow high-quality potatoes using agricultural techniques that have been found to produce the best possible yield.

On May 13, 2014, the first seeds of R12 potatoes, a variety known for particularly robust yields, were planted at the
Ramada Farm in the municipality of Une Cundinamarca
in the Eastern District of Colombia. This was a small proto-
type development project involving eighty-four people from
twenty-one families.

On November 11, 2014, the first Campo Vivo potato crop
was harvested. The agricultural and economic results were
even better than expected, including a productivity rate of
54.4 tons per hectare (over 130 tons per acre), well above the
national average of around 22 tons per hectare. Subsequent
crops have been equally successful.

Inspired by the experience of Campo Vivo, McCain came
up with the idea of creating a social business in France in
partnership with several other companies. It was called Bon
et Bien ("good and well"). It addressed a problem with which
the leaders at McCain were familiar for many years as a part
of their business, but which they did not think their business
had any special reason to pay attention to. Their involvement
in social business in Colombia changed all that. Their new
social business eyes noticed the problem and recognized the
opportunity it provided.

The problem I am talking about is unsold potatoes. It
turns out that in the conventional market for agricultural
products, farmers cannot sell 20 percent of the potatoes they
harvest because these potatoes are not of the proper shape for
making French fries or chips. They are not a good fit for the
machines used in the processing factories run by companies
like McCain. Another 6 percent of the crop remains under
the ground because ordinary harvesting machines miss these

potatoes. As a result, one fourth of the actual crop produced does not get to consumers—a major waste of food.

Potatoes aren't the only crop in which waste is common. Today, experts say that more than 30 percent of the food that we produce—an estimated 1.3 billion metric tons annually—goes uneaten due to waste, even as more than 800 million people suffer from hunger and malnutrition. At the same time, the world's population is forecast to grow from 7 billion to 9.6 billion during the next thirty-five years, placing our agricultural resources under even greater pressure. It is therefore simply unacceptable to waste food that could be consumed.

Food waste occurs for many reasons. It happens at every phase of the food industry value chain, from harvest through storage, transportation, preparation, and service, all the way to consumption, due to a variety of specific factors at each stage. But the ultimate underlying cause is our dysfunctional economic system, which decrees that any product that can't be sold for a price that will generate at least an industry-average profit must instead be discarded or destroyed.

Isn't it odd that we don't feel any responsibility for this—that we don't feel obliged to look for any solution for this problem? Thirty percent of the vegetables produced in Europe are wasted for a strange reason—because they are born with irregular or even "grotesque" shapes. They are known in the business as "ugly vegetables." They do not fit into the perfect military formations we see in supermarket displays, and so they are rejected, although they are perfectly edible and full of nutritional value.

McCain created Bon et Bien to tackle this longstanding problem. They brought other partners into the venture, including five members of the International Food Waste Coalition, an association of food companies dedicated to avoiding food waste: retailer E.Leclerc, recruitment experts Randstad France, the food banks of France, and the French Potato Growers Association (GAPPI). Each of these groups offers a unique contribution to Bon et Bien. In October 2014, they launched the company to convert the ugly vegetables into attractive food.

Here's how Bon et Bien works: McCain teams up with some of its one thousand regional growers to collect supplies of fresh but ugly vegetables. The vegetables, including potatoes, carrots, chicory, and onions, are then transformed into a variety of soups, in accordance with recipes provided by local chefs. (Simply chopping the ugly vegetables into pieces eliminates the main barrier between the consumers and the delicious, nutritious food, since the consumer has no way to find out what shape they originally had.)

The food processing workers who work at Bon et Bien have experienced long-term unemployment and are ready to reenter the job market. Randstad France manages the recruitment process and provides training and social support. The food banks of France take on an advisory role, and GAPPI acts as facilitator between the growers and the social business. Finally, the packaged soups are sold at Templeuve supermarkets (managed by the E.Leclerc retailing organization) using the Bon et Bien brand name.

Jean Bernou commented at the launch, "This project is a win-win solution for everybody. We are collaborating with our grower partners and a key customer, E.Leclerc, in the fight against food waste. At the same time, we are creating local employment opportunities and a source for potato flakes production in our factories. And all profit generated by Bon et Bien will be re-invested for the roll-out and increased social and environmental impact."[5]

Today, after more than two years of success, Bon et Bien is diversifying into production of ready-to-cook side dishes made from ugly vegetables. Bon et Bien is also expanding into Belgium and Greece, with Morocco to follow by the end of 2017.

Both Campo Vivo and Bon et Bien are addressing important SDGs, including number 1, No Poverty; number 2, Zero Hunger; number 8, Decent Work and Economic Growth; and number 12, Responsible Consumption and Production. Because they are sustainable businesses, they can be replicated without limit.

A New Economic System That Makes Human Goals Attainable

THE SOCIAL BUSINESS COMPANIES CAMPO Vivo and Bon et Bien opened up the blocked gates of innovation with new ideas. Many people around the world will come up with even more brilliant ideas than these. Since social business allows us to look at the world with new eyes, we can see things we could never see before. These new eyes will lead us to achieve all of the SDGs on time.

The SDGs define the key problems faced by the world today. That's what a global organization like the UN can do. Unfortunately, the moment the UN gets into explaining the processes by which these problems were created in the first place, it gets involved in a heated, never-ending debate. It's easier for me to volunteer my views as an individual.

From this perspective, I can explain that the list of SDGs does an excellent job of documenting where the mainstream economic system has failed us. You could describe it as a bill of indictment, listing all the charges against the existing system. Can we rely on the system that created all these problems to solve those same problems? Even if the problems do get solved, can we guarantee that the same system will not crank up the same problems all over again? Is there any logic to such thinking?

For this reason, I start with the premise that we must redesign the economic system to redesign the world. We need new roads to reach a new world. In a world where nonstop wealth concentration is viewed as the only legitimate economic activity, the SDGs cannot be sustained even if achieved. Neither can the three zeros—zero poverty, zero unemployment, and zero net carbon—which I've presented as my own, simplified version of the goals our civilization must pursue. To reach these goals, we need an alternative system based on concepts that are different and in which institutions and life purposes are different.

Social business represents a crucial element in the transition from our current greed-based civilization to a civilization based on the deeper human values of sharing and caring. It's a transition we must complete successfully if we want to pass along a truly sustainable way of life to the generations that will follow us.

PART
• • •
THREE

MEGAPOWERS FOR TRANSFORMING THE WORLD

7

YOUTH: ENERGIZING AND EMPOWERING THE YOUNG PEOPLE OF THE WORLD

FOR MANY PEOPLE, THE NEWS came as a shock. "A majority of millennials," the headline in the *Washington Post* reported, "now reject capitalism."[1] According to a 2016 poll of young adults between ages 18 and 29 conducted by experts at Harvard University, just 42 percent say they support capitalism, while 51 percent say they do not. This was just the latest survey to show the grave distrust many young people feel toward the mainstream economic system. For example, a 2012 survey by the respected Pew Institute found that while 46 percent of millennials have a positive view of capitalism, 47 percent have a negative one. Journalist Max Ehrenfreund described the Harvard results as reflecting "an apparent rejection of the basic principles of the U.S. economy."

This was surprising, to say the least. In 1991, with the collapse of the Soviet Union, it had seemed as if the only viable challenge to capitalism had died. What has happened that made the younger generation turn against the capitalist system that had apparently emerged triumphant just twenty-five years earlier?

Defenders of the sacred free market responded with surprise and dismay. Economist Michael Munger, writing on the website of the Foundation for Economic Education, seemed to regard the poll results as meaningless, saying, "It's not clear that you can 'reject' capitalism, any more than you can reject gravity."[2] Some commentators pointed out that the young people polled did not embrace any clear alternative to capitalism; just 33 percent said they supported socialism, for example. Others emphasized the fact that the survey respondents were given no clear economic definitions to apply, and speculated that perhaps the poll results simply reflect confusion over what "capitalism" really means.

Perhaps the best comment was offered by Sarah Kendzior, writing in *Foreign Policy* magazine. "Is it any wonder over half of 18- to 29-year-olds in America say they do not support capitalism?" she asked. Kendzior went on to say:

> You do not need a survey to ascertain the plight of American youth. You can look at their bank accounts, at the jobs they have, at the jobs their parents have lost, at the debt they hold, at the opportunities they covet but are denied. You do not need jargon or ideology to form a case against the status quo. The clearest indictment of the status quo is the status quo itself.[3]

I was not surprised by the survey results. My work takes me to college campuses all over the world. I have many opportunities to speak with young people about their lives, the challenges they face, and their hopes and dreams for the future. It has long been obvious to me that young people everywhere, in the wealthy countries as well as in the poorer nations of the world, are deeply dissatisfied with the social and economic system they are inheriting. They are vividly aware of its shortcomings, not simply because of the difficulties they personally are experiencing—unemployment, student debt, diminished opportunities—but because of the global problems they see around them, from the persistence of poverty and environmental destruction to rampant inequality and violations of human rights. However, I don't think they understand clearly that all the problems they see around them are because of capitalism. I think they are simply saying that they don't like what they see around them. Most important, they do not regard "the system" as sacred, nor do they believe that the outcomes produced by the free market are always perfect, as some ideologues insist. They judge the system by the results it produces, and on that basis they consider it flawed.

On the other hand, most of today's young people are not embracing any of the alternative ideologies once proposed as replacements for capitalism, such as socialism or communism. They view those systems as equally flawed. Instead, they are eagerly seeking a new approach—a new set of structures that will reflect more accurately the realities of human nature and have the potential to liberate the creative powers of people to solve the serious problems faced by humankind. I notice one thing that is common in today's young people: they are more willing to be useful to others than previous generations. They are looking for ways to make themselves useful to the world.

The polls show only that young people are unhappy with the system—that it is not delivering the results that could keep them satisfied. To put it mildly, they don't feel inspired by the system. They may or may not be actively searching for a new economic system. Some feel trapped within the walls of structures like the stock market or traditional monetary and fiscal policies. They greet anybody who offers to let them breathe fresh air outside these walls with cheers. This explains the enthusiasm I've encountered when explaining my ideas to youthful audiences on every continent.

The young people of today are the ones who will lead the world in creating the new civilization we desperately need. They are already hard at work, looking for ideas and an action agenda. Once they know what they want, they can achieve it much more easily than it could have been done thirty years back.

Today's youth are remarkably well equipped for any big task. Better educated than any generation in history, they are highly diverse and globally connected, thanks to the power of digital communication and information technology that is linking young people everywhere. International travel, student exchange programs and internships, and networking via social media have helped many of them to make friends across boundaries of nationality, race, and religion.

Today's youth have only a blurred picture of what kind of world they want. However, they realize that both the academic world and the political world have failed to give them a road map to the better world they want, nor have they provided the tools they need to design a road map of their own.

Their frustrations push them in two different directions. Some tend to become pessimists and withdraw from society, while others still hope that things will take a turn for the better. They feel they have enormous power, but cannot figure out how they will use this power. Any convincing map of the future that connects with their inner hunger will galvanize them into an unstoppable force the likes of which the world has never experienced before.

As an integral part of the education system, I propose that every year each class should spend one week imagining the broad features of a world they would like to create if they were given the freedom to do it. For the first two days, they should collect and review the list of features of the world each student has individually imagined. Then for the rest of the week they should work together to produce one or more agreed lists of features of the world they think is right for them.

Today, students are never told that they can create a world of their own. But I think that imagining such a world should be the most important part of the education process. Once they design this world, they will start thinking about how to translate it from imagination to reality. If we can imagine something, there is a good chance that it will happen. If we don't imagine it, there is almost no chance of it happening. In designing their imaginary world, the students will realize how different the current world is from the world they want. That realization will be the beginning of activism.

Today's young people represent one of the three "megapowers" that I believe will transform global society in the next few decades, by redesigning the economic structure completely to unleash the creative power of women and men everywhere. They will make sure that the system does not remain an elegantly designed machine for producing a handful of wealthy, world-dominating elephants, leaving billions more to spend their lives as working ants. Once today's youth know clearly what kind of world they want, making it happen will be so much easier.

Schools and Universities Can Enable Young People to Design Their Own World

As I've explained, one of the core problems of the existing economic system is the assumptions and attitudes we instill in young people during their education. We raise our children to

believe their lives begin with jobs. No job, no life—this message is sent loud and clear from every direction: home, school,
media, political debates, everywhere. When you become an
adult, you offer yourself to the scrutiny of the job market. A
job is your destiny. If you miss it, you show up in the bread
line. Nobody tells young people they are nature-built to become entrepreneurs rather than waiting in line to get hired.

Another important lesson our young people learn as children is that the fundamental purpose of work is to generate
personal income and wealth. We teach them that all other
motivations, including unselfish desires such as the drive to
help others and to make the world a better place, are of secondary importance and are only to be pursued in one's "free
time," or to "give back" as a kind of repayment. Based on
these assumptions, young people are led into narrow pathways
that restrict their areas of activism and achievement. They remain satisfied with little things, forgetting about their innate
capability to pursue global dreams and make them happen.
If we wish to create a new civilization that recognizes, hon-
ors, and empowers the broader range of human desires and
abilities, we need to change the educational system and the
assumptions behind that system.

I am happy to see a new development on various university campuses around the world. In the past ten years, many
universities have added social business courses to their academic programs. There is a growing network of university
programs in countries around the world where professors and
students are researching, studying, experimenting with, and
learning about new ways of organizing and growing economic
activity.

Now universities located in all continents are establishing Yunus Social Business Centres (YSBCs) to teach courses,

undertake researches, and to act as clearing houses for social business ideas for business leaders, foundations, NGOs, social activists, government organizations, financial institutions, and so on. Some of these centers hold social business design competitions to find social business solutions for problems that students identify on their campuses, in their nations, and even around the world. Graduate students are accepted in these centers to undertake deeper research on various aspects of social business. Social business academia conferences are held regularly in November in various leading cities of the world. Research papers are presented, and new programs and experiences are shared through these conferences.

As a result, an increasing number of young people are developing the tools and insights they need to put new forms of economic thinking into practice, and to spread the new ideas even more widely in the future.

On April 9, 2017, an agreement was signed by the Yunus Centre to establish the newest of these university centers at Lincoln University in Christchurch, New Zealand—the thirty-fourth YSBC in the world. Others are located at Glasgow Caledonian University in Scotland; La Trobe University Business School in Melbourne, Australia; Becker College in Worcester, Massachusetts; the University of California at Channel Island; the Chinese University of Hong Kong; King's College in London; National Central University in Taiwan; Renmin University in Beijing; the HEC business school in Paris, France, and in Montréal, Canada; the University of Florence, Italy; Azerbaijan State University of Economics (UNEC); the Asian Institute of Technology in Khlong Luang, Thailand; a group of universities in Barcelona, Spain; and various other institutions around the world, from Germany to Japan, Malaysia to Turkey. More centers in other regions of the world are already in the pipeline, and in the coming months the number of YSBCs will exceed fifty.

As you can imagine, each of these Yunus Centres is unique, drawing on the special strengths of the individual university partner, the interests and issues most important to the local and national economy, and other distinctive characteristics. For example, our centers at Glasgow Caledonian University and at the University of New South Wales have a special focus on health care issues, especially as related to the medical needs of poor people like those living in underprivileged neighborhoods in urban Scotland and Australia. The YSBCs at Kasetsart University and Lincoln University have a focus on agriculture. The YSBC at SSM College of Engineering in Tamil Nadu in South India has a focus on social business opportunities for graduate students in the engineering and technology disciplines. In other locations, Yunus Centres may focus on industries, agriculture, manufacturing, or services, depending on the needs and resources of the institutions.

Despite these variations, all of the university-based Yunus Centres have certain activities in common. Each can be considered a kind of think tank for issues related to economic innovation and social business, focusing particularly on poverty alleviation and sustainability, conducting workshops, seminars, conferences, and other meetings to discuss the latest research and developments in the field. Each develops courses on social business and other forms of economic innovation for both students and entrepreneurs. And each acts as a hub to facilitate exchange of ideas among academics, business leaders, entrepreneurs, and government officials.

The HEC business school in a southern suburb of Paris illustrates some of the varied ways universities are advancing and promulgating knowledge about economic innovation. The co-founder of the HEC Society and Organizations Center is Professor Bénédicte Faivre-Tavignot, who is also holder of the university's Social Business/Enterprise and Poverty Chair.

Dr. Faivre-Tavignot has helped to spearhead a series of projects related to economic innovation at HEC. The university now offers a social business certificate to students who complete a prescribed course of study and research. It also sponsors an online educational program (a "massive open online course," or MOOC) called Ticket4Change, which has so far helped to train around forty thousand students in the techniques and strategies involved in being what Faivre-Tavignot calls "entrepreneurs of change." In addition, HEC offers an executive education program for practicing business leaders under the title of Inclusive Business and Value Creation. Finally, all of these forms of research and learning are linked by HEC to experiments in real-world business development through the French Action Tank, whose work I described in Chapter 3 of this book.

Other universities that are part of the Yunus Social Business Centres network have developed their own curriculum and training offerings. Glasgow Caledonian University offers a Master of Science (MSc) degree in social business and microfinance. The Yunus Social Business Centre at the University of Florence organizes annual "days of formation" that introduce more than a thousand university and high school students to the concepts of social business. At a number of universities, such as the La Trobe Business School, modules on social business have become part of the required curriculum experienced by all students.

Many of the Yunus Centres are also actively promoting economic experimentation by working with practitioners and entrepreneurs on social business projects. For example, the Yunus Social Business Centre at Becker College is partnering with existing and new nonprofit organizations in the surrounding communities to launch and grow social businesses. In partnership with Millbury National Bank, it has also created a microcredit program to provide loans for startup social businesses in central Massachusetts, with special emphasis on projects being launched by Becker College students or recent graduates.

As these examples show, there's an enormous worldwide demand among young people for information and ideas about social business and other forms of economic experimentation. The youth of the world are uncomfortable with the current economic system and frustrated over the lack of an escape route from it. It is a hopeful sign to see how educational institutions across the globe are responding to the needs of young people by offering them options.

Whether the social business concept will take root in the economy or become merely a forgotten form of idealism practiced briefly by a few enthusiasts will be decided by young people on the university campuses and by the universities themselves. I am happy to see their enthusiasm growing and the eagerness of universities to create YSBCs in their campuses. The maturity of these centers will be reached when bachelor's and master's degrees in social businesses are offered, and when Action Tanks are a standard feature in the cities where these centers are located.

Younger students at the high school and elementary school levels also need to be involved in the change. Programs aimed at accomplishing this are now beginning to emerge. In June 2016, experts from Grameen Creative Lab helped lead an educational program that reached more than ten thousand

European high school students. Financed in part by the European Union (EU), this workshop engaged students from 373 schools in seven countries, who worked with 507 teachers and more than 200 business consultants to master the concepts behind social business and develop project ideas of their own. In fact, a total of 668 social business ideas were generated during the program. Even more impressive, 97 percent of the students who took part say they are hoping to launch social businesses in the future.

The educators involved in the workshop are planning to build on the experience. For example, they expect to create a permanent "social entrepreneurship ecosystem" that will encourage continuing study and experimentation with new economic models within European high schools. They also hope to develop a student evaluation system that could lead to the creation of a formal certificate of entrepreneurial competencies. Credentials like this are not important in themselves, but if they encourage more teachers and students to get excited about social business and the entrepreneurial path to economic and social progress, I am all for them.

We need many more programs like this workshop throughout the world and beginning with students even younger than high school age. A broader understanding of economics—one that recognizes the selfless side of human nature as well as the selfish side, and acknowledges the many varied motivations, beyond personal enrichment, that drive human creativity and productivity—needs to be inculcated in young children from an early age. We should tell our daughters and sons that they can be job seekers or job creators, and that they should prepare to make this choice. We need to encourage girls and boys to dream big dreams—to imagine the kind of world in which they'd like to live, and then to plan specific projects and businesses they can create that will help to make that imagined world a reality.

YOUTH IN ACTION: THE EMERGING GLOBAL NETWORK OF SOCIAL BUSINESS ENTREPRENEURS

TRAINING PROGRAMS IN SCHOOLS AND colleges can play an important role in energizing young people to help transform our economy. But thousands of young people around the world are not waiting for traditional educational institutions to lead the way. Many are teaching themselves about social business, seeking out peers who are already engaged in economic experimentation, and making new discoveries about themselves and their potentialities in the most powerful way possible—by just doing it!

One example is MakeSense, a technology-based organization that serves social business in a variety of ways. It was founded by a young man named Christian Vanizette who has an interesting personal story. Originally from the South Pacific island of Tahiti, Vanizette was trained in science and engineering and spent his first years after university pursuing a successful career in high technology. He was making a good salary and steadily earning increased responsibility and power when one day the company CEO called him into his office to explain the next project he wanted Vanizette to undertake. He told Vanizette he would be spending the next several months working for a client, figuring out how to connect refrigerators to an electronic communications network—part of the growing digital phenomenon known as the Internet of Things.

Vanizette found that he was troubled. He knew that this would be an interesting and challenging job from a technological standpoint. But he wondered about the practical social benefit it would generate. The more he thought about it, the less meaningful it seemed. "There has to be a better way for me to use my abilities than teaching refrigerators how to talk to one another," he decided. So Vanizette shocked his family and friends by quitting his high-paid job. He'd realized that he wanted to learn more about a new idea he'd heard about somewhere—an idea called social business.

Vanizette took his savings out of the bank and undertook a round-the-world trip to learn about social business. He met with many entrepreneurs from Asia and Africa to Europe and the Americas, investigated social and economic problems in many countries, and got to know the needs and desires of countless poor people and others grappling with major life issues. After several months, he came up with an idea that he thought would help make a valuable connection between his high-tech knowledge and the many varied opportunities he'd discovered for social businesses. That was the germ of MakeSense.

Christian Vanizette and his friends around the world have now become a strong force behind the social business movement. Over twenty-five thousand young people now participate in MakeSense, offering ideas and support for social businesses in countries around the world. I'll tell about MakeSense—and particularly about its use of technology to help spread social business—in more detail in Chapter 8.

Another example is the growth of Yunus&Youth (Y&Y), another international organization of young people dedicated to social business. Co-founded by Cecilia Chapiro, an energetic young woman with extensive experience in both the business world and the nonprofit arena, Y&Y started when a group of people from around the world came together at the Global Social Business Summit in 2013 in Kuala Lumpur, Malaysia, to connect with leaders in social business. The attendees saw a huge potential: What if the current generation of social business leaders shared what they know with the next generation of social entrepreneurs? Y&Y was born from that insight. Its central purpose is to provide eager, ambitious young social business entrepreneurs with the guidance, advice, and support they need to turn their dreams into practical realities.

Today, Y&Y has offices in the United States, Brazil, and Morocco. The organization is led by a global team of young professionals from eight countries and from many different walks of life—graduate students and consultants, journalists and graphic designers, including people who have worked for Google, McKinsey & Company, and Grameen Bank, along with Rhodes and Fulbright scholars, engineers, and poets. Their chief mission is to identify, recruit, and incubate some of the next generation of social business leaders. Young people who are selected to become Y&Y fellows are guided through a unique curriculum that teaches them lean startup principles that help them build successful social businesses that are sustainable and strategically sound.

Over a six-month period, Y&Y fellows attend biweekly webinars given by business experts, connect with a global network of change-makers and professional mentors, and receive relevant content and personalized support from the Y&Y team. Fellows are also matched with professional mentors— successful entrepreneurs and business professionals ready to lend their expertise to help the fellows maximize the growth potential of their social businesses. These early-stage startups drive social change because their founders are close to the problems they're solving and the communities they're helping.

The 2016 class includes twenty-six Y&Y fellows from seventeen countries. They include the following:

- Diego Padilla from Peru, the founder of Recidar, a social business based on a reutilization model. Recidar collects reusable objects from homes, resells them at low prices in poor communities, and uses the sales revenue to launch capacity-building projects. Diego's goal: to create a solidarity chain that connects people with other people and nature through reducing waste and creating entrepreneurial opportunities in low-income communities.
- Walaa Samara from Palestine, who created Bella Handmade Jewelry, which works on empowering and providing job opportunities to women in refugee camps. Walaa's dream is to provide a source of hope to women living in devastating conditions and give them a means to make a living for themselves and their families.
- Hendriyadi Bahtiar from Indonesia, who founded Sahabat Pulau, a social enterprise that works on bettering the lives of fishermen's wives through production of a fish-based Indonesian national snack. His long-term vision is taking 22 million Indonesian women and their families out of poverty and bringing them to an income level of at least US$3 per day.
- Jezze Jao from the Philippines, who created the Carrier Pigeon Project, a fashion e-commerce social business whose proceeds are used to fund educational scholarships and literacy programs for underprivileged Filipino children. Jezze's goal: to use education

as a key enabler for individuals to rise above their present circumstances and have a chance at pursuing their dreams.

MAKESENSE AND Y&Y AREN'T THE only organizations that are helping young people embrace the power of social business. Another is Social Business Youth Alliance (SBYA), a global initiative that has been in operation since 2013. SBYA teaches young people about social business through training programs, workshops, and competitions. It also creates opportunities for promising young social business entrepreneurs to meet with potential investors, thereby overcoming one of the big hurdles that company founders face—getting access to capital with which to launch their enterprises.

One of SBYA's activities is Social Business Champ, a social business plan competition designed for university-level students to showcase their entrepreneurial skills and creativity to generate solutions for pressing social problems. Another is YY Goshti, a hub for social business incubation. The YY Goshti Innovation Camp involves an intensive training program where selected participants receive sixty hours of training and participate in exposure visits to see how existing businesses function. This development process culminates in a public event where the participants pitch their social business models in front of an audience of veteran entrepreneurs, investors, and stakeholders, including social business fund operators like Spark International (based in Australia) and the Blue Gold Program (sponsored by the government of the Netherlands). The winners then enter a three-month-long Startup Operations session, in which they are provided with office space, mentorship, and other essential resources required to run their social businesses.

SBYA also holds periodic summit meetings that bring together young people from around the world who are excited
about the potential of social business. These gatherings are
among the most powerful activities that SBYA sponsors. As
explained by Shazeeb M. Khairul Islam, president of SBYA,
"We bring 300 bright minds together at one eventful hub for
two days of exciting networking opportunities. Participants
from universities, social businesses, startup communities, in-
cubators, accelerators and various social business funds are
coming together to discuss the possibilities and challenges
that face social business today. It is the 'complete package' because we are offering access to knowledge, human resources
and possible funding prospects."[4]

A final story about young social business entrepreneurs
is that of Impact Hub. I had a pleasant surprise visiting this
remarkable organization's Berlin location, Impact Hub Berlin, most recently in April 2017. I was the chief guest in the
launching ceremony of its parent organization, Impact Hub
Vienna, in 2010. I had no idea how it had grown since then.
I found Impact Hub Berlin an impressive place—a bright,
colorful building that includes a meeting room, an innovation
lab, an event space, a focus area, and a cafe area. All are designed to let young social business entrepreneurs gather, swap
ideas, share stories, learn from experts, and tackle challenges
together. Leon Reiner, the managing director of Impact Hub
Berlin, has developed an attractive menu of events and services that budding entrepreneurs find inspiring.

Impact Hub has come a long way from its origins. Back in
2005, it was founded by Jonathan Robinson, a young entrepreneur and writer, under the name of Hub on the top floor of
an old warehouse in London. Its goal was to help local youth
pursue the path of entrepreneurship. Robinson did not create

Hub as a business, let alone a social business. He only came to know about social business much later, when he had a chance meeting with Hans Reitz of Grameen Creative Lab on a flight in 2009.

Robinson's interest got a further boost when he was approached by Hinnerk Hansen and two other young entrepreneurs who wanted to set up a version of Hub in Vienna as a social business. Jointly they reconceptualized Hub and made plans to expand it through franchising. They gave the company a new name—Impact Hub—and a new headquarters in Vienna. They created the Impact Hub Association, a collective of all present and future Impact Hubs, and made it the sole owner of the Impact Hub Company, a charitable company with the mandate to manage global operations and facilitate the development of the network.

Hans Reitz helped arrange funding through a newly formed social business fund called Good Bee, established with Reitz's advice by the Vienna-based Erste Bank and the Erste Foundation. I had the honor of formally launching Impact Hub Vienna in 2010.

Today, there are eighty Impact Hub locations in forty-five cities around the world, including London, Vienna, Melbourne, Johannesburg, Sao Paulo, San Francisco, and Singapore. Impact Hub serves over fifteen thousand members who are building innovative businesses with social goals in almost every imaginable arena, from poverty, health, and women's empowerment to energy, education, and the environment.

The worldwide enthusiasm behind organizations like MakeSense, Yunus&Youth, SBYA, and Impact Hub illustrates the appeal of social business to young people the world over. The challenge of creating a new civilization doesn't frighten today's youth—they are energized by it!

Athletics—A Celebration of Youth,
and a Force for Social Good

WHEN I WAS INVITED BY Thomas Bach, president of the International Olympic Committee, to address the committee's annual meeting in Rio the day before the opening of the 2016 Olympic Games, I saw an opportunity to remind the leaders of the global sports world that athletics are a celebration of youth—and a potentially powerful force for change.

I've always looked at the world of sports with awe. What an enormous impact it has. Thrilling events like the Olympic Games captivate the attention of billions of people from all corners of the planet.

At the same time, sport is an integral part of human life. Every child in the world starts his or her life with sports, usually self-designed, without rules, coaches, or training. Kids gather to create their own games, impose their own discipline, and have unlimited fun doing that.

As children grow up, some of them stay with sport, while others move away from it. But the spirit remains, continuing to energize people, though often going unrecognized. Sometimes we create a glass wall between the world of sports and the world of everyday lives. People from both sides see each other, but they don't cross the wall. I feel strongly that both worlds will be enriched if we remove the glass wall, creating one world shared by basic human beings of various orientations and differing degrees of athletic skill, but all experiencing the joys of play, achievement, and friendly competition.

Because most people love sports, athletes have enormous influence on their fans. Business leaders recognize this, which is why they use athletes and sporting events to promote their products. The same power can be used to encourage sports fans to use their tremendous creative powers to address the problems the world is facing.

One way the sports world can mobilize fans to tackle social issues is by creating social businesses at the club level, the district level, and the national and international levels. These businesses can focus on issues like youth unemployment, health care, education, and technology, just like any other social businesses. They can also address some of the many problems of the sports world itself—for example, the challenges that athletes face when their relatively short careers end and they must switch to another life after their intensive period of competition is over.

These days, we talk about the legacy programs left behind after major sports events like the Olympics. Such programs can and should include social businesses created to help in preparing for the games. Social businesses can be involved in building stadiums and pools for the games, constructing housing for the athletes, and providing food for all the participants. These and other social businesses can be designed to produce streams of benefits for people on a long-term, sustainable basis.

In the same way, there can also be legacy programs for each club, each team, and each event in the world of sports, no matter how modest. Athletes and fans alike will feel good to know that they are participating in something that gives them enjoyment while playing a positive social role. Since sports is about competition, each club or association can bring the spirit of competition to their approach to social problems. Think of the pride that the athletes, their fans, and an entire community can share when their favorite team has not only won a league championship but, more important, has helped to bring housing, better schools, or affordable health care to thousands of people in need!

I was delighted that my speech before the International Olympic Committee in Rio drew a very positive response from most of the members of the committee. It has also led to some concrete and immediate actions.

Right after my speech, Anne Hidalgo, the mayor of Paris, invited me to dinner that evening. During the dinner, she made it very clear that she wants social business to take root in Paris, with sports playing a leading role.

Later, I visited Paris to discuss these ideas with her further. Mayor Hildalgo held a press conference at which she dedicated Les Canaux, a historic building in the nineteenth arrondissement of Paris, to serve as Social Business House. I was formally invited to set up Yunus Centre Paris in this building to promote and coordinate social business programs in the city. The mayor went on to say that if Paris is chosen to hold the Olympics in 2024, she intends to make those games the first Social Business Olympics in history. But whether or not Paris is selected, she intends to continue to pursue the goal of making Paris the world capital of social business.

In the months since then, Mayor Hidalgo has taken a number of steps to achieve this objective, including having young people in Paris organize social business design competitions to address the problems of the city. Mayor Hidalgo is also the chair of C40, an association of global megacities that are committed to combatting the problem of climate change. Today the association has a membership of ninety cities with a combined population of 600 million.

After this experience with Mayor Hidalgo, I cannot say that the world's political leaders are not listening to the demands of young people for economic and social change. Some definitely are.

Intergenerational Partnering: How Young and Old Can Work Together to Create a New World

You can see that I am very excited about the potential of the world's young people to help lead the transformation of the global economy that humankind so desperately needs. But, of course, this doesn't mean there is no role in the project for older people like me. In fact, I think there is amazing potential to be realized from a powerful alliance between generations—young and old combining forces to create a new civilization that will serve the needs of all humanity.[5]

Now that I am in my seventies, I am often asked my opinion about the worldwide demographic trend toward an aging population. Usually this is couched in terms of a serious economic and social challenge. As people live longer, there is a need to take care of a growing number of elderly people. How will society cope with this difficulty?

I was recently asked to address this so-called aging problem while on a visit in Germany. My friends in the country had arranged for me to conduct a TV interview with two aged people and speak to them about what they are doing, what they can do, and their thoughts about the aging problem.

On the interview day, they surprised me by bringing in two ladies who were both over 100 years old. One of them—I'll call her Helga—was 105 years old. She narrated stories from her past, including the time she got into a fight with Adolf Hitler. A leader of the Communist Party, she was jailed many times; during one jailing she was set up to be murdered, but she escaped.

Helga remembered every detail of her experiences flawlessly, right down to specific people, places, and dates. At one point, when I urged her to write a book, she replied, "Young man, I have written twenty-eight books, do you want me to write another one?"

To change the subject, I asked her how she feels about young people today. She immediately replied, "The less I talk about them, the better. They think they know everything. They have no interest in listening to anybody."

I asked whether she was making these observations on the basis of her personal experiences with young people.

"Of course. I have a daughter and she drives me nuts. She is impossible."

I asked, "How old is she?"

"She is seventy-five," Helga replied calmly.

Suddenly I realized that the word *young* means different things to each of us. I found myself wondering how we can possibly force people to "retire" at age sixty-five. To Helga, a sixty-five-year-old is practically a baby!

I think Helga has the right attitude toward aging. For a number of years now, I have been urging that we retire the word *retirement*. As they get older, many people look at their approaching retirement date as a dreadful day. It is taken as a message from the working world saying, "Good-bye—you are no longer productive, useful, or creative." Many of those who have retired don't know what to do with themselves. For these people, retired life appears like a punishment.

Whether an employer should keep a person working after a certain age is his or her business. I do not want to question that. My serious objection is to using the word *retirement* for this particular transition point in people's life. What a terrible word it is! It tells you to close down your working life. I do not understand why anybody should be forced to retire, except for health reasons. Society has no business retiring people. An employer has the right not to employ a person after a certain age, but not the right to declare someone unfit for work by declaring it a retirement. Can a human being be mothballed? Does it make any sense to think that people's creative power fades away or suddenly gets switched off because they cross a specific age limit? Do they suddenly transform into non-functioning, noncreative human beings the day they turn sixty-five? A person is not a machine with an on/off switch—a human being cannot be turned off.

For this reason, I insist that the word *retirement* should be retired from our vocabulary. We need a new word that acknowledges the continuity of creative life and emphasizes the opportunity to make a transition from phase one of life to phase two of life, the most exciting phase of life. Phase two is actually the freedom phase of life, when one is finally free from all the obligations of growing up and raising a family. This is the phase in which one can do all the things a person hopes to do, without interference from anybody.

A person approaching this transition should think:

> I worked for my employer for X number of years. Now that my contract is over, I can concentrate on doing things that I always wanted to do but could not get around to doing because of my job contract. From a walled world, I am entering into a world without walls—a wider world, a world of unlimited opportunities. Now I have an opportunity to be myself for the first time in my life. Now is the time to enjoy being me.

For all people, phase two of life is an opportunity to do things for the world. As it begins, such a person may say:

I've fulfilled my responsibilities to my employer, to my children, to my family. Now, at last, I can afford to devote myself to the wider world. This is the time when I can use my creative powers to solve some of the social problems that made me sick, to undo the things that are wrong, and do things I think should be done. I don't have to pay any attention to what others think—all that matters is following the instincts of my heart. This is my time for social business.

ONCE YOU BEGIN LOOKING FOR ways that older people can begin to participate more fully in the creative life of society, plenty of ideas for a better phase two pop up.

Another time on my trip to Germany, I was taken to a village in the state of Bavaria, by a Bavarian friend. It is a village of three thousand inhabitants with every possible facility for young people that a modern society needs—beautiful schools, beautiful gymnasiums, huge playgrounds. What my friend particularly wanted to show me was that the schools are largely empty, because there are not many children in the village—and based on current demographic trends, the situation is likely to become more extreme.

On the other hand, the village has a steadily rising population of people age sixty and older. Most of them are bored, lonely, and at loose ends; many spend their time at the pubs, drinking and becoming depressed.

My friend arranged for me to meet with some of the villagers, and we had a long and intense conversation. Together we decided that a new program should be launched in the village. Everyone over age sixty will be invited to enroll in the schools to learn how to start their lives all over again. While studying new topics they never had a chance to think about before, they'll also get to interact with the children who are there. Utilizing the excess facilities of the schools to give new inspiration to the unused, experienced human resources may produce exciting frontiers of action—including amazing opportunities for young and old to learn from one another, creating a new social chemistry.

The idea of forging partnerships between young and old can also spark new solutions for the problem of financially supporting our growing population of elderly people. Phase two is not only a time to devote yourself to addressing social problems, but also a good time to create a social business trust or fund. The money in such a trust can go to support the creation or expansion of social businesses. You can put the bulk of your savings into your trust and manage it yourself, telling your children and friends that they will have to manage it when you are gone. One does not have to be wealthy to create a social business trust or fund. You can do it with whatever money you have that you do not need now, or you can create it after your death through a simple provision in your will.

To get a sense of the potential of this idea, just look at all the existing pension funds around the world. They amount to an estimated US$25 trillion, all continuing to grow through investment income and new contributions every year. What a gigantic financial force, all devoted to the welfare of old people! If we invest a fraction of this money in social businesses to solve the problems of old age, for the poor and the rich irrespectively, all those problems can be addressed in short order. Old people will no longer be a social problem or a social burden anywhere.

Old people are creative, resourceful people. It's time we recognized that, and liberate our elderly people to contribute as much as they want to the work of transforming our society. We must escape our old ideas about old people. We should treat them as creative people with freedom to dedicate themselves and their wealth to creating the world they always wanted.

8

TECHNOLOGY: UNLEASHING THE POWER OF SCIENCE TO LIBERATE ALL PEOPLE

WHEN I SPEAK ABOUT THE need to transform the world and create a new civilization that can accommodate all the human values while solving the biggest problems facing humankind, I sometimes get pushback from people who believe that technology will solve our problems. They point to the amazing scientific breakthroughs that have been achieved in recent decades and say, "Experts in technology will be able to fix everything. Global warming, hunger, lack of health care, problems with education, income inequality—all will be solved by the amazing new products and services that researchers will develop in the years to come." Some predict an era of abundance in which everyone on Earth will be showered with riches. You'll be able to get anything you want, anytime and anywhere you want it, just at the touch of a button.

This is supposed to be the inevitable outcome of the incredible advancement of science that the future will bring.

I am a big enthusiast about the potential of new technologies. I assign technology a central place in making massive social and economic improvements in the world. But I don't believe technology will fix everything automatically. Technology can work wonders. But we must remind ourselves that technology does not have a mind of its own. Technology is a tool designed for a purpose—and that purpose comes from human beings. We decide the purposes for which we design technology, and we decide how to adapt it for other purposes.

People are the designers and drivers of technology. In today's world, it is designed mostly for selfish purposes, for commercial success—and sometimes even for terrible destruction, as the history of warfare shows clearly. The real challenge now is to allow social designers and social drivers to take the reins of technology and guide it in the direction we need it to go.

Since I am not a technology designer, I have been trying to adapt available technology designed for selfish purposes to give it a social purpose. But this is only a second best. Technology designed for social purposes to begin with would be more powerful and would create its own exponentially expanding positive force. We are still missing that development in technology. I have been trying to draw attention to this gap through my work of adapting existing technology for social purposes. Let me explain a couple of examples of this process of adaptation.

Years ago, I became a strong believer in the power of information and communication technology (ICT) to change the lives of poor people. This encouraged me to create a cell phone company called Grameen Phone. We brought mobile phones to the villages of Bangladesh, and we gave loans to poor women so they could buy them for income-generating purposes. They became the "telephone ladies" in the villages, selling telephone services to the villagers. This created a new form of entrepreneurship. When we launched Grameen Phone, the local telephone lady was often the only person in the village with access to modern communication technology. Local people who needed to make a link with the outside world—to get connected with urban markets, to get information from a government office, to get a health update from a relative in a distant village, or to say hello to a family member living in the United States or working as a migrant laborer in the Middle East—would rent a few minutes of cell phone time from the telephone lady.

This simple entrepreneurial business model became an instant success. Nearly half a million poor women in Bangladesh made extra income for their families as telephone ladies. Today, cell phones are so common throughout Bangladesh that the heyday of the cell phone ladies is past. But they made telecommunication a well-appreciated household technology for every family in the entire nation in a very short period.

Renewable solar technology is another area in which amazing breakthroughs have been occurring. I took advantage of this technology to solve an age-old problem of the rural people of Bangladesh by creating a social business company to bring solar home systems to rural people in an affordable and reliable way. As I explained in Chapter 5, Grameen Shakti has become a very successful company by developing and marketing solar home units, biogas units that convert animal waste products into fuel for heating and power, and environmentally friendly cookstoves. All are priced within reach of most rural families in Bangladesh.

Some may wonder why we found it necessary to start businesses to bring cell phones and renewable energy technology to the poor people of Bangladesh. Since these technological marvels were originally brought to market by traditional profit-maximizing businesses, we could have waited and let them address the needs of the rural poor in Bangladesh.

The reason we chose a different path is very obvious. Conventional businesses have different goals than ours. They go where the money is. To make the most money, one markets products to the people at the top of the income ladder—preferably the 1 percent who control most of the world's wealth. If the ultrawealthy are out of reach, the second most attractive opportunity for making money is offered by the large middle class. However, although the bottom of the wealth structure includes a massive number of people, it commands an insignificant wealth base—which means it is not an attractive area for making profit. This is why technology tends to arrive at the bottom of the pyramid only after businesses have exhausted the markets above them.

By contrast, organizations like the Grameen family of companies go to the bottom as our priority area. That's where all the social and economic problems are. That's the area where social businesses must rush in. Social businesses design products to cover their costs while solving a problem, not to hit the financial jackpot.

The more we advance in technology, improve our infrastructure, spread globalization, and bring efficiency to the economic system, the more intensely global corporations focus their strategies on competing to serve the wealthiest and the middle class. If you work for a conventional business, you won't choose to design a smart phone for the poor until you've exhausted the markets in the upper layers of income. And when you do, you'll simply make a cheaper version of your existing product rather than designing a phone specifically to meet the needs of the poor—one that would not only be cheaper, but also simpler, upgradable, exchangeable for the next model, extremely durable, and more efficient in addressing poor people's needs.

It is interesting to note that new technology products are never launched in the poor segment of the market and then gradually adapted to higher-level markets. It is always the other way around. The result is a big gap in the technology marketplace—one that billions of people around the world have fallen into.

The latent power of modern technology is definitely awe-inspiring. Every year seems to bring new breakthroughs. Technologies that bring new levels of speed, flexibility, and power to activities like transportation, manufacturing, agriculture, health care, and especially to information management and communication are revolutionizing many industries. But there is no global vision driving these changes. Great innovations are designed and dedicated mostly for commercial successes. Creativity rushes in the direction where businesspeople see market potential.

A technology genius always has two basic options. For example, he can dedicate his work to creating a medical breakthrough that will save thousands of lives—or he can develop an app that will let people amuse themselves. In most cases, the technology genius will be pushed to focus on the product that has the potential to create millions of dollars in profits. Profit is the North Star of conventional economics. Lacking a collective destination, the only highway sign we follow is the North Star of profit. Nobody is putting up any highway signs that will lead the world toward a collectively desired destination. It raises the question, does the world have a destination? If not, should it?

As I've explained, the Sustainable Development Goals (SDGs) are an attempt to define an immediate destination over a very short period. They represent a good beginning. The SDGs give us a destination over a fifteen-year stretch—just a moment in time out of the human journey of hundreds or thousands of years. Many people and institutions have made commitments to travel in the direction that the SDGs reveal—but, unfortunately, most for-profit companies are not redirecting themselves in meaningful ways to reach those goals because the market definition of success does not include them.

Given the power of human creativity, especially as enhanced by today's amazing breakthroughs in technology, any destination is reachable. But while trillions of dollars are invested in developing robotics and artificial intelligence for military and commercial purposes, there is little interest in applying technology to overcome the massive human problems of the world. We gloat and float with our selfish personal goals and company goals. Lacking any social direction for technology, we are likely to miss the great opportunities that our selfish radars can't perceive.

However, there are individual efforts to bring the power of technology to achieve social goals. In countries around the world, individual people, company managers, nonprofit leaders, and social business founders are already at work developing ways to use technology for social benefit. Some of the results they have generated are impressive.

One example is Endless, a computer company founded by a young Californian named Matt Dalio. I know his father, Ray Dalio, a successful businessman who became very interested in my ideas and my work, and who provided the bulk of the financial support needed to launch Grameen America.

Matt Dalio was attracted to an idea that I talk about a lot—universal access to computers and the Internet. The computer is an all-powerful tool of creation. Once it is connected to communication technology, it can be made into a powerful solution machine. But most people in the world don't have access to this tool. Why? Because the computer is too expensive, and without connectivity it is not very useful.

Matt Dalio focused on these two issues. Recognizing the potential of computers linked to today's ICT to transform the lives of the poor, he set out to combine the power of the computer with that of the smart phone. He wanted to design desktop and laptop computer models from the ground up to be affordable and practical for users in the developing world, including people with little or no access to reliable electricity or Internet connections. He aimed at bringing down the price of a computer to US$50.

The cost of the technology itself did not pose the biggest challenge. Dalio knew that the same processors that power smart phones can power a computer's central processing unit (CPU). A keyboard and a mouse could be added for less than US$10. And most people have access to televisions that can be used as monitors. The biggest problem was connectivity. It could be summed up in two numbers: In emerging markets, the average online data plan provides for just 300 megabytes (MB) of data, while the average PC user consumes 60 gigabytes (GB) of data every month—about two hundred times as much. This means a typical PC is useless in these circumstances.

Dalio did not give up. Research showed him that communication itself is inexpensive. For example, it's possible to send 100,000 tweets on a 300 MB data plan. The real challenge is downloading information. But statistics show that we only consume a fraction of what is actually available online. For example, about 80 percent of Wikipedia searches focus on just 3 percent of Wikipedia contents.

That feature gave Dalio the opening he needed—data storage. Dalio has explained to me that most people can do fine with a much smaller storage capacity than we think. In practical terms, it is actually possible to take all of the images and data from every website the average person visits in a lifetime, compress them, and fit them onto a single 2-terabyte (TB) hard drive inside a computer. Result: It is possible to give an individual all the information he or she will ever need *without Internet connectivity.*

As Matt Dalio says, "The goal is not to have everything, but for everyone to have almost everything." This is the secret behind the amazing power of a low-cost Endless computer.

A typical Endless model runs on Linux, the open-source PC operating system, and comes preinstalled with fifty thousand Wikipedia articles and more than one hundred applications for education, work, and entertainment. The data supplied in this way can be used offline and gets updated whenever a link to the Internet becomes available. An incidental benefit is that kids who use Endless computers get access to almost all of the enormous information resources of the World Wide Web without being exposed to the risks of uncontrolled or unguided Internet use. Parents feel very relieved that they don't have to worry about how their children are making use of Internet access.

Most remarkable is the price: Endless computers sell for as little as US$79. The aim is still to bring them down to US$50 or less. But even the current price brings them within reach of many of the world's 4.4 billion people who formerly were unable to afford such a device.[1]

Endless has two types of businesses running in parallel. One part of Endless's business is operated like a conventional, profit-seeking company, while the other part is a social business that provides underserved populations with educational, health, and creative services they were once denied.

Endless is already being shipped around the globe by four of the five largest computer manufacturers. It has become the leading PC platform in Indonesia and much of Southeast Asia. It has also been selected as the standard operating system for the Brazilian Ministry of Education, and in coming months it will be adopted as the primary platform by a number of other Latin American countries. The Endless team is now developing tools that can educate any kid, anywhere, while also helping him or her learn to code—a skill that Dalio believes will be part of the basic literacy of future generations.

Given the amazing potential of the computer to transform the world, I think the brand name that Matt Dalio chose for his company is very appropriate. The opportunities are indeed endless.

You can probably see why I label technology the second megapower. It will play a critical role in helping us build the new world we seek—provided we harness it, not solely for the purpose of generating individual wealth or corporate profits, but in the service of all humankind.

Harnessing the Multiplying Power of ICT

When I launched Grameen Bank, one of the challenges we had to deal with was the lack of ICT in rural Bangladesh. Those were the days before the Internet, when few businesses in Bangladesh, and even fewer homes, were computerized, and when handheld devices like today's cell phones weren't yet born in the world. In the villages of Bangladesh, even access to electricity was a dream. The kind of digital record keeping and communication that modern financial institutions rely on today was completely unavailable.

Luckily, we did not have to worry about ICT, because at that time it did not exist. We designed our program for managing Grameen Bank using the means available. We relied entirely on meticulous recording of massive data by hand. It was quite a daring feat based on strong determination. We developed simple, low-tech systems to manage our accounting and management information system. Bank employees lived in the remote villages and reached the borrowers every day by walking long distances; riding bicycles on narrow, muddy roads or nonroads; or navigating the rivers that crisscross Bangladesh using tiny country boats. They recorded loan balances by hand in ledger books and reported to bank headquarters in Dhaka periodically.

The systems were slow and unwieldy, but they worked. We did not miss anything. And they were perfectly appropriate for us in serving borrowers who had never heard the word *bank* and had no idea what this animal was. Many not only were illiterate but had never even handled money before.

When desktop computers came to Bangladesh, Grameen Bank was the first institution to install them in its branches to store all its data. Since electricity was not available in the rural areas of Bangladesh where all our branches are located, we equipped the branches with generators. The idea of connectivity to the Internet was not an issue, since it did not yet exist.

Today, of course, Grameen Bank is totally computerized and networked using the most sophisticated accounting and management software designed especially for us. Staff members write almost nothing by hand, relying instead on automatically generated reports. Not only the staff but almost all of the borrowers and their children have cell phones, a good proportion of them smart phones.

With the world increasingly connected by technology, it's possible to do so much more, more quickly and easily, and thereby serve many more people. The new ICT has an amazing multiplying power: it enables businesses to bring services like banking into places that were extremely difficult to reach before. It also makes it possible to expand innovative social business programs to scale more rapidly than ever before possible.

One example of this multiplying power is the microfinance platform Kiva, a pioneer in the technique now known as crowdfunding. It was created in 2005 by Matt Flannery, a software writer, and his wife, Jessica Jackley. In 2003, when they were preparing for their wedding, Jessica took Matt to attend a lecture I was giving at Stanford University where Jessica was working. The story of Grameen Bank and our work with the poor women in Bangladesh moved them. After their marriage, Jessica moved to Uganda to work with a microfinance NGO. She found out that the limiting factor for reaching more poor people with microcredit is the lack of resources to give loans. This inspired Jessica and Matt in their own efforts to make capital available to those who would otherwise never obtain it.

The young people who visited us were millennials, which means they are "digital natives," raised to feel comfortable with technology. It was natural to them to think about how they could use ICT to multiply the impact of microcredit. The result was Kiva.

Kiva uses an Internet platform to connect entrepreneurs who need capital with others who have money to spare. Kiva allows individuals to lend money to others with projects they consider worthwhile, a small amount at a time—US$25, US$50, perhaps US$100 or so. The networking power of the Internet lets people make connections across vast geographic distances. And the instant data-crunching power of digital technology makes it easy to quickly find the kinds of projects you are interested in. If you want to lend money to a female entrepreneur working on an income-generating activity in Latin America—or a native craftsperson in Australia—or a woman selling snacks in the street in North Africa—you can probably find exactly what you are looking for on Kiva.

As a result, entrepreneurs who would not be considered creditworthy by a traditional bank are able to get financing for their small-business ventures. And individuals with small amounts to lend get the satisfaction of knowing that their money has helped to make a worthy new business into a reality. As of 2017, Kiva has connected 1.6 million individual lenders with 2.2 million borrowers in eighty-two countries through a global network of microfinance organizations. Kiva has facilitated loans totaling more than US$960 million, with a repayment rate of 97 percent.

When the concept of social business started taking root in many countries around the world, the idea of using the Kiva platform to support social businesses was a logical next step. Saskia Bruysten of YSB met Premal Shah, president of Kiva, and the two leaders brainstormed how to make it work.

The concept was first tested with two social businesses supported by YSB Albania. One is Rozafa, which manages fifteen artisan handicraft workshops in rural Albania, providing training, equipment, and sales and distribution centers, and providing income for over 120 local women. The other is E Jona, a café in the capital city of Tirana that caters to people with disabilities, providing them not only with drinks and snacks but with a place where they can comfortably get together and network.

When these projects debuted on the Kiva website, no one had any idea whether visitors to the site would understand the idea of social business, or whether Kiva would succeed in raising the money needed to support the businesses. Both fund-raising efforts were immediately successful. It was clear that the supporters of Kiva not only understand the social business concept, but love it. And, of course, the beauty of Kiva is that the global reach of the Internet means that social business projects anywhere in the world can be helped. YSB continues to use Kiva as a source of funding for selected social business projects in Albania, Haiti, Brazil, and Uganda.

Kiva was just the beginning. Now the powers of digital ICT are being used in new ways to multiply the effectiveness and reach of many other social business programs. An example is MakeSense, a youth movement launched by Christian Vanizette, whom we introduced in Chapter 7. MakeSense has two legal entities. One is a nonprofit dedicated to promoting social business, while the other is a social business legally designated as a for-profit company under French law. The latter company turns over any profits earned to the nonprofit that is its sole owner. This is what qualifies it as a social business, since it does not generate personal profit for any owner.

MakeSense operates an open-source digital platform in the mold of Wikipedia where thousands of individuals from around the world can freely interact with one another in creative, productive ways. The Wikipedia platform exists to facilitate the writing and editing of an encyclopedia of knowledge using information provided freely by thousands of volunteers; the MakeSense platform exists to help support the growth, development, and spread of social businesses.

The UN's seventeen SDGs are an important component of the MakeSense platform. If you are a would-be social business entrepreneur, you must start your work with MakeSense by explaining exactly how your project will directly support progress toward one or more of the SDGs. Once a MakeSense community developer validates the idea, information about your project becomes available on its website, along with a challenge you want to solve. The challenge could focus on a wide variety of business issues: "How can I identify the best possible market for the product I plan to make?" "What kind of distribution channels should I be considering?" "Where can I find a financial expert who might be willing to partner with me on this project?"

Now the MakeSense community, linked by the power of the Internet, springs into action. As of early 2017, more than 25,000 volunteers in forty-five countries use the MakeSense platform to make connections with over 1,300 social businesses seeking support. The volunteers call themselves Gangsters, while the entrepreneurs who are developing the social businesses are called SenseMakers.

MakeSense's online manual explains what the entrepreneur can expect to happen next:

> Then, people will start brainstorming and contributing ideas online and we'll put out a call for someone to facilitate a workshop based on solving your challenge in the next 30 days.
>
> Once a volunteer has stepped up to facilitate a workshop, you will get to choose a date and location for the workshop, and set aside an hour to discuss the details of your challenge with the facilitator.
>
> The volunteer who is organizing your workshop will use this one-hour interview to make sure that we are on

the right track with helping you tackle your most critical challenge. He or she will take into consideration your objectives and constraints to ensure you can implement the solutions to your business realistically. You will both agree on an output to make sure you are happy with the results of the workshop.

On the day of the workshop you will present your project to the participants. The participants will have a few minutes to ask you questions before the beginning of the creative process, which you will be invited to join. You will be asked to act like any other participant, to make sure the process develops unhindered by your approval or disapproval of their ideas.

After the workshop, please send a feedback email to the participants mentioning the solutions you liked, and tell them if you need help expanding on a solution or implementing it![2]

LIKE KIVA, MAKESENSE IS A powerful illustration of the multiplying power of ICT. When a social business entrepreneur posts a challenge on the site, he or she immediately has access to a worldwide network of consultants—thousands of people with experience, knowledge, and insights in fields ranging from advertising to human resources, programming to product design. Even more important, they are all enthusiastic supporters of the social business concept—people who are eager to help a new project succeed and start bringing benefits to those in need. Think how exciting and valuable this is, especially for a social business pioneer who may be working in a remote location or a poor community where business expertise is hard to come by.

MakeSense also serves as a hub for a number of other activities that are applying ICT innovation to the growth of social business. For example, it hosts SenseCube, a real-life (not virtual) incubator space for social businesses currently active in six cities: Paris, Mexico City, Brussels, Beirut, Manila, and Dakar in Senegal (West Africa). The focus is on projects that apply technology solutions and online communities to social business goals, with the objectives of using these tools to grow to scale faster and better than would be possible using only traditional means of communication.

An example of how this works is the Food Assembly, a business that links farmers to local people who want to order food for home delivery. The goal is to increase the incomes of small farmers and enhance their positive, sustainable impact on the local environment while also making healthful organic foods more widely available to city dwellers. And with the help and guidance of MakeSense, the Food Assembly is experimenting with using online networking to expand its services rapidly to many cities around the world.

Originally launched in the United Kingdom in 2014, the Food Assembly consists of a number of local businesses, each created and sustained by a host—an individual entrepreneur who is committing to the concept of sustainable local agriculture. Guided by expert facilitators from the Food Assembly Collective, the host finds a welcoming venue—perhaps a local park, community center, or school where regular food deliveries can happen—and recruits local farmers to produce the foods that will be offered. Then the host sets about building a local community around the project, using a variety of advertising, marketing, and publicity tools to attract customers who are eager to enjoy fresh-grown local produce. An online market is set up where customers can place their orders.

At a prearranged time (on Saturday morning, for example), farmers gather at the Food Assembly venue to deliver produce to their customers, who also get the opportunity to meet with the farmers who are feeding them as well as with neighbors who share their love of healthy, locally produced food. Over time, they often come to form a local community of people who join forces to support a variety of activities that express their shared values—for example, environmentalism.

As you can imagine, it would take a lot of time and effort to create a Food Assembly business one locality at a time. To jump-start the process, MakeSense has worked with the Food Assembly to develop a web-based platform that anyone can access from anywhere. Visit the site and you can locate the nearest Food Assembly. If there's not already one near you, you can learn all about how to join the movement, perhaps becoming a host or signing on as a producer. Participants from existing Food Assemblies are available to answer questions and provide encouragement. Thanks in large part to the attractiveness of this online platform, in less than three years, the Food Assembly has spread to more than seven hundred locations in France, Belgium, the United Kingdom, Spain, Germany, and Italy—a vivid illustration of what I mean by the multiplying power of digital ICT!

MakeSense is continuing to develop and refine its use of technological tools to enhance and spread social business. Beginning in 2016, a data scientist with expertise in developing and applying advanced analytic tools came to work at Make-Sense thanks to a grant from his main employer, the media company Bloomberg L.P. The scientist is working on a system to track and measure the performance of social business projects. The goal is to develop new, more accurate ways of determining which methodologies and practices produce the best results for the people whom the social business is designed to benefit.

USING TECHNOLOGY TO SOLVE THE UNIQUE
PROBLEMS FACED BY THE POOR

IN A WORLD WHERE TRADITIONAL profit-maximizing companies are driven by the need to continually increase revenues, profits, and share values, the needs of poor people naturally tend to be neglected by businesses. As a result, new technologies are normally quickly directed to creating products and services that people in the wealthiest nations and communities will find attractive. There is no shortage of video games, entertainment products, and other luxury items using new technology. But goods that tackle the challenges faced by the hundreds of millions of people struggling with poverty, hunger, homelessness, and other problems are in short supply.

Fortunately, a growing number of social businesses are exploring ways to adopt technology to address the problems of the poor. In some cases, they are taking technologies originally applied to high-priced products and services sold to the rich and finding ways to simplify and redesign them to work for the poor. In other cases, they are developing entirely new products from the ground up based on intensive study of the life circumstances of the poor. These projects are beginning to make the truly transformative potential of new technologies into a reality.

Consider, for example, Agriculture and Climate Risk Enterprise Ltd. (ACRE), a technology-based social business whose mission is to provide smallholder farmers with protection against natural risks, primarily through innovative insurance solutions. I've come to know about ACRE because it is supported, in part, by an investment from Grameen Crédit Agricole's Social Business Fund. This is an investment fund created by Crédit Agricole, a giant network of French banks originally created to serve the nation's farming communities. The fund is dedicated to investing in social business companies and is primarily oriented toward developing countries, with special attention to Africa. (I'll say more about this fund in Chapter 11.)

Launched by the Syngenta Foundation for Sustainable Agriculture in June 2014, ACRE is designed to address the problem of economic risk that particularly plagues small farmers in Africa, making it exceedingly difficult for them to work their way out of poverty. To understand how it works, you first need to know a little about the realities of agriculture risk and how the problem is normally addressed.

Farming, of course, has always been an inherently risky business. Weather is impossible to control and difficult to predict, and it has a huge impact on the crop yields that farmers depend on. In addition, uncontrollable and unforeseeable shifts in the local, national, and global markets for agricultural commodities can cause wild swings in the price of farm goods. These can easily wipe out a farmer's profits for an entire season overnight. Yet farming is an essential industry. Humans are absolutely dependent on it for survival, and no society can afford to take chances with its food supply. So most countries take steps to protect their farmers from the economic risks inherent in agriculture.

This is why, in many countries, including the United States, agricultural insurance is made available to farmers at prices subsidized by government support at up to 60 percent of the cost. However, these subsidy programs only cover large-scale farmers and the insurance policies they purchase. In this respect, as in many others, small business owners are usually not viewed as creditworthy or bankable—which means they have no access to financial tools that larger business owners can take for granted.

Thus, "microinsurance" plans that would be appropriate to small farmers are not eligible for subsidies—even in regions like Africa, where small farmers represent a huge portion of the agricultural industry as well as the population. The main reason is cost: Administering insurance policies is expensive, and when a policy is small, the relatively high cost makes it difficult to provide coverage at a reasonable price. It's a problem that affects some 450 million small farmers (those with plots of land less than 2 hectares in size) throughout Africa and the rest of the developing world—farmers who support families that number more than 2 billion people in total. In Kenya, for example, more than 96 percent of agricultural land is rain-fed and vulnerable to drought and erratic rainfall, putting farm families at constant risk of being wiped out economically.

ACRE uses technology to address this problem. It has created the first insurance program designed to serve smallholder farmers using mobile technologies and up-to-the-minute climate and agricultural data to make coverage effective and affordable. ACRE's team of thirty local and international specialists based in Nairobi, Kenya, conduct computerized analysis of historical data on weather and crop yields that enable them to develop customized insurance products using mobile technology. Recent breakthroughs in satellite weather forecasting and monitoring technology have also played a key role in making the necessary data available.

The result is the largest agricultural insurance program in Africa, marketed in Kenya under the brand name of Kilimo Salama. To make ACRE's insurance affordable and widely available, they've bundled it with other products that farmers are already buying, such as microcredit loans and even packages of seed or fertilizer. The process of getting insurance is very simple. A packet of seeds contains a small card describing the indexed insurance policy the farmer is entitled to receive, including a number he or she can call to activate the insurance. Insuring 1 acre of maize against drought typically costs a farmer around US$37, which is about 10 percent of the value of the harvest—a modest price to pay for protection against a drought or flood that could wipe out the entire crop.

Then, based on the weather results for the next several weeks, the experts at ACRE can automatically determine whether the farmer is eligible for an insurance payoff. It's not necessary for a representative of the insurance company to visit the farm to validate the need for a payment. This reduces costs dramatically and enables the insurance business to provide far better service to its customers. Depending on the policy, the payout may be as simple as a new supply of seeds provided to the farmer without cost, or it could be an automatic cash payment received by the farmer's digital bank account on his or her cell phone.

By the end of 2015, nearly four hundred thousand African farmers had been covered by ACRE's insurance technology. It's a remarkable example of how modern ICT is able to solve problems of poverty that once seemed insoluble—provided the technology experts and business managers are able to set aside concerns about profit and concentrate on developing simple, practical solutions that meet the needs of poor people.

As I explained in Chapter 3, one of the hopeful signs that new economic awareness is spreading around our world is the interest shown by some of the most successful corporate leaders in experimenting with social business alongside their traditional profit-maximizing operations. One of the companies engaged in this effort is Intel Corporation, the Silicon Valley–based firm that is a worldwide leader in manufacturing computer processors and other advanced high-tech products.

The birth of the effort that became known as Grameen Intel took place following a visit by Craig Barrett, then the chairman of Intel, to Bangladesh in 2007. Barrett and I met and talked at length about the Grameen family of businesses and the concept of social business. After much thought and discussion, Barrett and his colleagues decided to create a social business whose focus is using technology in creative ways to help the world's impoverished people find a path to a better life. Funding for the project has been provided by Intel Capital and Grameen Trust, which are the two shareholders in the social business.

Today, Grameen Intel has an office in Dhaka, Bangladesh, as well as team members based in the United States and India. Some work full time for Grameen Intel, while others are Intel employees who devote a portion of their time to the social business. A range of projects are under development, centered on software applications devised to address specific problems of the poor. Most are designed for use by compact, portable computing devices such as smart phones, which are affordable, widely available, and very suitable for use throughout the developing world, from rural villages to crowded big-city neighborhoods.

Some of Grameen Intel's initiatives are aimed at improving the productivity and profitability of small farmers, the same group supported by the ACRE insurance program. For example, Mrittikā is an app that provides farmers in remote villages of Bangladesh with the most up-to-date and accurate information on soil quality, plant nutrients, and fertilizer requirements—with remarkable benefits for entire farming communities.

Mrittikā works in conjunction with widely available soil testing methodologies that measure the level of basic nutrients likc nitrogen, phosphorous, and potassium, as well as pH (acidity) levels. The genius of the app lies in its ease of use and in the thoroughness and accuracy of the information it provides. With a few keystrokes, the app user can enter complete data about the farmer and his or her plans, from the precise location of the field (using Google Maps) to the proposed crop, the planting season, and much more. In response, Mrittikā offers detailed guidance as to the kinds of fertilizers recommended, the exact amounts to use, the ideal dates for application, and so on. The app even provides a list of local supply stores where the right fertilizers are available for purchase at competitive prices. As a result, farmers can buy and use the appropriate fertilizers, and no more—which saves money, improves crop yields, and protects the long-term health of the soil, which is easily compromised by overuse or misuse of chemicals.

Grameen Intel performed extensive tests using demonstration plots to verify the accuracy of the app's recommendations. The results were compelling. For example, a test crop of eggplant (a popular food in Bangladesh, locally known as *begun*) produced higher yields using the fertilizer recommendations provided by Mrittikā when compared with either the traditional methodologies passed on through generations by Bangladeshi farmers or the official standards provided by the government-run Bangladesh Agricultural Research Institute (BARI). What's more, the fertilizer regimen recommended by Mrittikā cost 29 percent less than the BARI recommendation and fully 468 percent less than the traditional method—a potentially huge saving for a typically cash-strapped small farmer.

Today, Mrittikā is in use in forty locations in Bangladesh and is also being tested in India and Cambodia. The app is popular among local entrepreneurs who offer soil analysis services to farmers using chemical testing kits in combination with the app. Thus, Mrittikā not only benefits the farmers but also helps to support the ancillary businesses of those who advise farmers as well as those who sell fertilizers, providing a welcome boost to the entire rural economy.

Health care is another area in which poor people have special needs—needs that many traditional profit-maximizing companies may not consider it worthwhile to address. Grameen Intel is also working on solutions for some of the unique health problems of the poor.

One of the biggest problems faced by poor people, especially in the developing world, is simple access to health care information. Rural villages where millions of people live are often many miles away from the nearest hospital or clinic, and dirt roads and lack of efficient transportation systems can make a twenty-mile trip into a bone-jarring all-day journey that no person in ill health should have to endure. Local doctors and nurses fill the gap to some extent by making house calls. But there aren't enough professionals to meet the demand, so countless poor people go for months or years without ever having the opportunity to consult with a health care expert.

Modern ICT can help alleviate some of these problems. One of Grameen Intel's projects in this area is aimed at providing health care information to expectant mothers, many of whom have no access to prenatal treatment. In June 2017, Coel will become available—a smart, wearable bangle made of high-quality, durable plastic that provides prerecorded messages with advice and guidance about maternal health. The design is extremely clever: Coel works for ten months without requiring a battery charge, which means it will last through a woman's entire pregnancy. It works without Internet access, speaks whatever local language the woman uses, and flashes an LED alert whenever it has a message to deliver. It can also be timed to an individual user's due date so that it provides appropriate health care information and advice at the right moments; there are some eighty health messages to be delivered at a rate of about two per week.

Coel's benefits don't stop there. The bangle is also designed to monitor and test the quality of the air that its female wearer is breathing. In particular, it can detect indoor air pollution, particularly carbon monoxide, which is often generated during cooking with fuels like wood, charcoal, or dung. Millions of women in Bangladesh and other developing countries inhale such dangerous fumes every day, often with dire health consequences for their babies. Coel will provide alerts when this is happening so that women will know it's time to step outside for fresh air.

The work that Grameen Intel is doing to develop technological solutions to some of the most serious problems of the poor is tremendously promising—and inspiring. What's more, they are not the only ones working along these lines.

One of the most ambitious health care technology projects I know is being led by Dr. Ashir Ahmed of Kyushu University, one of the institutions that has partnered with me and the Grameen family of businesses to create a Yunus Social Business Centre. Dr. Ahmed labels his project the "Doctor in a Box." It's a portable collection of diagnostic tools, together with a display and communication interface, that can be used by a doctor, a nurse, or a trained health care assistant when visiting a village or an individual patient's home. Armed with this kit, a health assistant can transmit data to a physician in a distant city who can respond with specific diagnostic information and treatment recommendations.

Perhaps most intriguing, Dr. Ahmed believes that once his Doctor in a Box is in use, it will encourage outside companies to provide goods and services that will enhance the usefulness of the service. He writes, "This box will create opportunities for medical equipment vendors to design and develop diagnostic tools, and for software vendors to structure these diagnostic tools in such a way that a nurse with a minimum of training can operate." Over time, the power of the Doctor in a Box may grow dramatically, including many specific tests and tools tailored to the health care needs of people living in particular countries and regions.

Dr. Ahmed's brainchild, which he estimates can be made and sold at a cost of about US$300, is already being tested in Bangladesh. He foresees a day when millions of these kits could be used by nurses and assistants throughout the developing world, helping to address the unmet health needs of billions of people.

• • •

We live in a challenging era—a time when population growth, rampant inequality, environmental degradation, and other problems are posing serious challenges to the future of the human race. Yet it's also a time when human capacities have been expanded like never before, thanks in large part to the amazing technological developments that science has made available over the past few decades. If we build the new economic and social system needed to channel these technologies in the right directions, there is every reason to believe that this phenomenal megapower can play a big role in turning the world of three zeros from a dream into a wonderful reality.

9

GOOD GOVERNANCE AND HUMAN RIGHTS: KEYS TO BUILDING A SOCIETY THAT WORKS FOR ALL

A THIRD MEGAPOWER THAT WILL be crucial in creating the new economic system humans need to survive and thrive is a political and social structure that minimizes the problems of corruption, injustice, and potential tyranny, and that respects the rights of all people.

Some people have mistakenly believed that respect for human rights and the need for economic growth and development are two unrelated issues—or even that these two imperatives are somehow in conflict. This is a mistake that was made in the old Soviet Union, where harsh acts of political repression were sometimes justified by the need to forcefully grow the Russian economy, the better to compete with the West. But economic growth built through ruthless government policies is not sustainable growth. The essence of entrepreneurship is in people's ability to unleash human creativity to the maximum. It cannot germinate in an environment of repression and harsh government control.

Countries that are taking the path of autocracy in the belief that this will lead to economic growth are likely to be disappointed in the long run. It's far better to establish an atmosphere of freedom and experimentation in which the creative energies of individual entrepreneurs are unleashed. This is how vibrant communities are nurtured—and how nations with shared, sustainable economic health are built in the long run.

Fortunately, most economists, political theorists, and social scientists now accept this principle. The intimate connections among good governance, human rights, economic justice, and economic growth are now widely recognized. The challenge is to put this understanding into practice—to establish economic, political, and social systems that consistently honor the principles of freedom, justice, and integrity, and thereby unleash the potential for creativity and growth among people from every sector of humankind.

Like all big challenges, this will be hard to achieve. It will take wisdom, discipline, selflessness, and courage. But no challenge we will face as a species in the next half century is more important than this. Good governance is essential no matter what we want to achieve in taking our society forward.

We need to meet a number of specific requirements if we hope to unleash the crucial megapower of good governance and human rights in pursuit of our goal of a transformed world. They include fair, credible elections; corruption-free administration of the government; an honest, civil society sector; and respect for the rule of law. In the pages that follow, I'll elaborate my views on these and other essential elements of good governance.

Fair and Credible Elections

It's impossible to have an honest, well-run government unless the legislators and the highest executives of government are chosen through elections that are unmanipulated, free of intimidation, and worthy of popular acceptance. Thus, to a large extent, the quality of national elections determines the fate of good governance. If elections are not conducted using fair, transparent procedures, none of the other components of good governance has any chance.

In a democracy, a national election represents a kind of filter whose repeated use can cleanse the politics and governance of the country. But if this filter is clogged, there's little chance of having a government worthy of the name. When elections are rigged, you are likely to end up with a government that is in reality an oppressive, plundering machine—one whose chief goal is to make sure the filter remains clogged forever.

Holding elections in an environment of complete trust in the system is a basic foundation of good governance. Every voter should feel that his or her vote counts, and that he or she can choose candidates freely without any threat of intimidation or reprisals. It is not easy to hold such elections in many countries.

Unfortunately, the world tends not to pay much attention to the quality of elections. A national election is often regarded merely as a ritual that each country has to go through, or dismissed as an "internal matter" that no outside party has any right to comment on.

Yes, an election is definitely an internal matter, but the quality of elections should be a concern of other nations, too. A fraudulent election leads to an illegitimate government and thereby vitiates the community of nations. A manipulated election can install a government that may destabilize the country, threaten the region, and promote activities that are harmful to the world.

For these reasons, I strongly feel that the United Nations should give a very high priority to promoting credible elections, making this a part of its peace and security agenda. It should have a special program under this agenda to develop appropriate technology to hold credible elections, to provide continuous technical support to all election authorities, and to monitor and report on the quality of all national elections. Since the quality of elections is so closely tied to the quality of government itself, ensuring high election quality is important for regional and global peace and security, as well as for achieving the SDGs and the objectives of all the specialized agencies of the United Nations, such as the UN High Commissioner for Human Rights, UN Women (dedicated to gender equality), UNICEF (children's rights), UNDP (economic development), and WHO (health care).

The UN should develop an array of political and technological tools to help ensure this. For example, the UN could develop unbiased systems for grading the quality of elections. It could use these systems to rank countries, individually or in groups of countries, in order of election quality, and to provide financial, political, and diplomatic benefits to countries that steadily improve the quality of their elections. It should assess the independence and integrity of the officials who manage election machinery as well as the level of freedom enjoyed by the press, the opposition parties, and national and international watchdog organizations. Based on these and other measures, the UN should establish standards to define a minimum acceptable quality for elections, and impose sanctions on countries that repeatedly fail to comply with such standards. Regional associations of nations can play a valuable supporting role in encouraging member states to live up to the UN's election standards.

The UN can also play a valuable role in developing and promoting improved forms of voting technology, including application of the latest information and communication technologies. Leading ICT companies—the Googles, Facebooks, and Twitters of the world—can be invited to help design these new voting technologies and to work with the UN in demonstrating them. For example, the UN could sponsor the development of a technology that enables remote voting through smart phones using biometric identification tools. This technology could help solve the problems of voter intimidation and violence at or near polling places, which discourages millions of people from participating in elections.

At the same time, making it possible for citizens to vote over a period of time—a week or a month rather than on a fixed day—from home, office, or anywhere in the world, could dramatically increase voter turnout. The latest ICT tools to facilitate instant tracking through live vote counters (like Worldometers, which reports, among many other statistics, the world population as it grows every second) could provide information on the number of votes received by various candidates as voting continues. This running information could encourage greater voter enthusiasm, excitement, and participation. Voter indifference may disappear if a voter sees that a "wrong" candidate is attracting lots of votes, while his or her own favorite is falling behind. The best way to activate voters is to make the election a highly publicized *live* event over several days so that everybody knows how the voting is going at each moment, and each voter feels that he or she has a chance to participate and influence the result.

As global standards for improved election methods are developed, the UN can play a year-round role in assisting and
monitoring national governments in preparation for elections.
An election is not an isolated event taking place on a certain
date; it is the end result of a long process. If the process does
not proceed right, the end result cannot be right. In cases
where the process is flawed or corrupt, watchdog organizations led by the UN should be ringing their warning bells to
make the nation, and the world, aware of what is about to
happen. This will make it possible for corrective steps to be
taken before an illegitimate election undermines the credibil-
ity of a national government and threatens the safety of the
entire community of nations.

Corruption Is the Killer Disease

THE NEXT BIG ISSUE THAT threatens good governance is corruption. Sometimes, the problem of corruption is minimized
by people who say, "All countries, including rich countries,
have corruption—no country is immune from it. So why
make a fuss about it?" Some people even cite examples of
countries that supposedly flourished through corruption, as if
to imply that corruption is merely a way to "grease the wheels"
of society and make it run more smoothly.

It's true that corruption is a widespread problem. There's
corruption at a personal level in practically every society, including isolated corruption scandals in countries that are economically advanced and relatively honest. In many countries in
the developing world, corruption is endemic—so thoroughly
institutionalized that citizens have given up on protesting
against it and instead have accepted it as part of their lives.

In these countries, corruption is the killer disease of good governance. It's easy to point to the shocking figures regarding public money channeled to corruption every year. But this is only part of the story. Even more disastrous is the way corruption destroys the whole governance system. The level of corruption directly determines the level of the rule of law. If one can use money to buy any government decision, national policy, or court verdict, the rule of law becomes a mockery. And when political power means a free ticket to wealth, people will commit any crime to get that power, which is one of the reasons why election campaigns in many countries are so often accompanied by violence.

It's disheartening to see how political corruption has become increasingly sophisticated in recent years. Corrupt governmental leaders and their business partners have learned to use smart public relations techniques to explain away the evidence of their crimes through impressive fairy tales—what some are now calling "alternative facts"—that they spread through their control over media and their allies in the intellectual community. They make the public believe that anyone who opposes them is a traitor deserving to be put on trial. In this way, they tighten their grip on power and make their own corruption even harder to uproot.

Once a culture of corruption has taken hold, it tends to spread to every level of society. Anybody who works for the government comes to expect a bribe for every service he or she provides—a kind of "personal fee" on top of the worker's regular salary. To justify the fee, ensure its payment, and extort additional money, the worker becomes innovative about designing difficulties for citizens who need service. The payment demanded for simply verifying someone's ID or accepting a filled-out form may be small, so to increase his or her income, the worker makes things more difficult for the citizen. Some officials let it be known that they can offer big-ticket services that will make impossibles possible, giving clear indication that no law or rule can stand in the way. Hard-to-get business licenses, competitive government contracts, favorable tax rulings, lenient court decisions—all are available for the appropriate deal. And if you complain about the price, your friend in the bureaucracy has an answer ready: "I know this seems expensive, but it can't be helped. The money has to be split with all the higher-ups in the chain, right up to the minister who is the final boss!" In the biggest deals, the minister negotiates directly with the "customer."

Besides these in-house negotiations, political corruption often extends to include countless agents outside the government who call themselves consultants, advisers, agents, lobbyists, representatives, management service providers, and so on. "Crony capitalists" who are friends, relatives, or financial partners of powerful politicians claim the most lucrative contracts for infrastructure and other projects. A huge share of the national income is diverted to this "corruption sector." The cost of every government contract or project is inflated to account for kickbacks and other kinds of wasted money. The result is that the public gets poor-quality infrastructure, supplies that are not usable, and government services that create health hazards or even risk lives.

The weaker the rule of law becomes, the higher on the scale corruption rises—and vice versa. The biggest danger of autocracy is that it leads to limitless corruption around the big boss. When the head of the government becomes corrupt, the disease becomes an unstoppable epidemic eating away the fundamentals of the society. Every basic institution, from the judiciary and the police to the military services and the financial system, becomes dysfunctional. Often they are converted into tools of repression to ensure that those in power continue to reap their ill-gotten rewards.

Minimizing government corruption and crony capitalism is not an easy challenge. History shows that, where money and power are combined, human behavior tends to become corrupted. National and international laws and treaties that forbid corruption in business deals have not accomplished their goals. Too many companies continue to violate the legal and ethical standards set by their national legislatures; practices like money laundering and offshore harboring of cash gained through illegal activities continue to flourish.

Periodic scandals in the United States and other Western countries show that no system is immune to this problem. But despite the scandals, some societies have a better overall track record than others. It makes a difference when clear rules against self-dealing, conflicts of interest, and nepotism are written into law and then enforced, strictly and fairly.

Creating a society where honest government is the norm rather than the exception needs a national commitment and well managed institutions. Many elements play a role. Autonomous power centers within government are important—for example, an independent judiciary that can hold officials to account when they violate the law. Strong civil society institutions outside government, such as independent newspapers, civic watchdog organizations, nonpartisan community organizations, and respected colleges and universities, can play a useful role in exposing corruption and calling for corrective action. And government leaders themselves must set an example of selfless, patriotic service, thereby helping to create the expectation that public servants are working to benefit all people, not to enrich themselves or their friends.

Global corruption watchdogs like Transparency International (TI) have been doing a commendable job in drawing public attention to corruption country by country. I particularly like TI's Corruption Perceptions Index.[1] I would like them to add another index that will complement that index—an Election Perceptions Index. Looking at both indexes together, people will be able to see the relationship between the two and prepare to take political action whenever needed. They can realize that improvement in one area will also bring improvement to the other. I hope TI will consider this proposal.

The world must continue to insist on strenuous efforts to stop corruption in the day-to-day functioning of governments. Otherwise, we will continue to pay a terrible price in terms of failing to build a society on the basis of good governance.

Government Is Not the Problem

I hope I am not giving the impression that "government is the problem," or that the solution is "less government" or even "no government at all." People are the government, and the government is the people. Without government, we do not exist as a community or as a nation. The government's job is to translate the vision of the people into reality in the best possible way. At the same time, government is the leader of the people. Its role is to keep the economy and the society moving in the right direction. Government is so important in our lives that we cannot turn our eyes away from it. We want it to be good, we want it to be ideal, we want it to be perfect—and the closer to perfect it is, the more it can approach becoming invisible.

Government certainly can't take the place of individual entrepreneurs. But history clearly shows that well-run governments have an important place in helping societies unleash the creativity of entrepreneurs. The societies that have been most successful in reducing poverty, improving the average standard of living, protecting a healthy environment, and encouraging the personal development of ordinary citizens have been those with strong, stable, honest, and efficient governments.

Some of the countries of Western Europe, North America, and East Asia are examples of this pattern. They are not perfect, but generally they are trusted by their people, despite enormous disagreements between people and the government. People are usually confident that they have clear avenues of recourse to resolve those differences. Have the governments of these countries sometimes faltered in their commitment to honesty and fair dealing? Of course. Have they made mistakes that have hindered economic growth, permitted the persistence of poverty, and tolerated the rise of excessive inequality? Again, yes. But some of the traditional characteristics of these countries, including their overall respect for the rule of law, their general support for economic freedoms, and their tendency to be responsive to the needs of citizens at all levels of the social ladder, have been important factors in their economic success.

By contrast, some of the countries of the Global South, where these values are less widely respected and practiced, have faltered in their quest for economic progress. The difference is unmistakable, and it underscores the importance of good governance—not as a replacement for individual initiative but as an essential support.

OTHER IMPORTANT ELEMENTS OF GOOD GOVERNANCE

OTHER SPECIFIC ELEMENTS OF GOOD governance that I consider vital to creating the new and better economic future our world needs include the following.

Investments in infrastructure that support economic growth. Some of the essential resources needed to launch successful businesses—whether they are traditional profit-maximizing businesses or social businesses—are beyond the capacity of individual entrepreneurs. If you can come up with a great idea for a product or service that thousands or even millions of people could benefit from, that's wonderful! But turning this idea into a successful enterprise will be difficult if the social and economic infrastructure that surrounds you is inadequate. When the roads connecting villages, ports, and cities are in bad shape; when the bridges and tunnels that cross rivers and pass through mountains are crumbling or nonexistent; and when there are no decent airports or shipping ports to facilitate the movement of goods and people from one city to another, then building a successful business and growing it to scale is extremely slow, costly, and hard.

In building and maintaining infrastructure, government has an essential role. Some vital forms of infrastructure may not yield enough revenue in the short run to be economically self-sustainable. In such a case, government agencies supported by taxes and fees need to step up to the task. Over the long term, if the projects are well designed and managed, they will help generate economic vitality and growth, producing more than enough revenue—including tax collections—to pay for themselves. This is what happened with infrastructure projects in the United States such as the Tennessee Valley Authority, which brought electric power to the poorest communities in the rural South, and the Interstate Highway System, which connected the entire country with a network of efficient, high-speed roads, helping to fuel the rapid economic growth of the 1960s and 1970s.

Now public-private partnerships are providing an increasingly popular structure for building infrastructure. Here a private company or consortium partners with the government to create a highway, a tunnel, a subway system, a power plant, or an airport. The details vary, but in general, the private sector makes all the investment on the condition that it receives exclusive right over the management and income generated by the investment over a lengthy specified period, usually twenty-five years or more.

Unfortunately, there's always a danger that infrastructure projects can be misused to enrich politicians and their friends rather than to benefit the community. Mega infrastructure projects that are politically very attractive while also creating the potential for giant kickbacks to the decision makers offer a safe, convenient path to corruption for government officials. Greedy, corrupt businesspeople have refined these secret deals to make them so difficult to uncover that the politicians involved are made to feel absolutely immune to any public scrutiny.

This is where the vital elements of good governance come into play. Emerging countries historically lacking in infrastructure need to build modern facilities in order to participate fully in the global economy. The citizens simply must insist that essential resources of good governance be put into place to minimize the waste and injustice that corruption produces. There's no substitute for diligent scrutiny from civic groups, watchdog agencies, and nonprofit organizations in making this happen.

Using technology to enhance government efficiency and transparency. In the private sector, we are both excited and worried about the potential of such new technologies as robotics, machine learning, and artificial intelligence. We are excited because of the efficiencies they will produce, while we are worried because of the job losses and the economic dislocations they may bring.

Yet while we debate the impacts of these technologies in the private sector, I urge their adoption in areas like government services and global finance, particularly in countries and regions where corruption makes the lives of ordinary citizens miserable. I believe that encouraging governments to replace bureaucrats and officials with robots, artificial intelligence, platform networks that give people access to vital data, and well-designed software algorithms can help make governments more efficient, people-friendly, and corruption-free. When people can use a smart phone app or a web page to download information from government databases, to submit forms for permits or licenses, to lodge complaints about failed government services, or to request assistance with community problems, the problem of corruption can be sharply reduced. The power of official gatekeepers who demand bribes before they'll open the doors of government can be greatly weakened, making it easier and more pleasant for people to get access to the government help they need and deserve.

Good governance shouldn't depend on the rare circumstance of having only ethical leaders in the government. We can use technology to reduce the opportunities for self-serving officials to twist government to their own benefit.

Incorporating social business in civic projects. Some government programs, such as infrastructure projects, can be designed as social businesses. For example, in my book *Creating a World Without Poverty,* I explained how big infrastructure projects like a mega port can be built through a social business corporation owned by the poor people of the area.[2] If we make public demands that governments give priority to social businesses in selecting companies for all purchases and contracts, big or small, it will reduce the involvement of greedy profit-maximizing businesses in public affairs.

One risk is that unscrupulous owners of profit-maximizing businesses will start creating fake social business "front" companies to compete for government contracts. However, even if this happens, matters won't be worse than before. Close scrutiny by independent watchdog groups and journalists can reduce the problem. And over time, genuine social businesses will grow to outcompete the fake ones.

Social business offers a sustainable way for governments to fulfill one of their central responsibilities—namely, to take care of people at the bottom of the economic ladder and to open up opportunities for them so that they can take care of themselves and live with dignity. Most of the time, this responsibility is addressed in an unsustainable way through the provision of state charity. In some cases, government handouts to the poor are necessary, but they should not be seen as a permanent solution to the problems of poverty. A permanent solution should be one that does not take away the initiative and dignity of the people who need to be helped. Since poverty is not caused by the poor but rather by the system we have created around them, government's primary job is to fix the system and to put in place a process by which wealth concentration gradually reverses itself, creating a society where the wealth of the nation is shared by all. As I've argued throughout this book, social business can help make this happen.

Running financial and business organizations should be avoided by the government. Keeping them in government hands makes good governance more difficult and creates temptations for politicians in government, in collaboration with other officials, to use these enterprises to promote their personal and political purposes. As soon as possible, government-run enterprises should be transferred to non-government hands, preferably by creating social businesses delinked from government. When transferring these assets, governments have to be extra cautious that they don't hand them over to greedy hands. As we've seen in many countries, transferring assets to personal-profit-driven private ownership is another thriving avenue of corruption.

Involving poor people themselves in planning and executing development projects. A crucial element in increasing the chances for good governance is to give ordinary people a strong voice in the decisions that affect their lives. In the case of developing infrastructure to boost economic growth, for example, this would mean giving poor people the opportunity to participate in shaping the plans for infrastructure projects.

We've set an example for this kind of decision making at Grameen Bank, where the board of directors is made up of women who are borrowers from the bank and at the same time owners of the institution. Elected by their peers, the board members participate fully in policy making of the Grameen Bank.

Some people seem to assume that giving poor people authority over decisions that impact their lives is a foolish or impractical idea. But the arguments that could be made against this kind of participatory decision making are mostly insignificant. Poor people may lack certain forms of knowledge that are useful in designing infrastructure projects. But when it comes to making policies and decisions that impact their lives, they are the top experts around the table. In such situations, their wisdom and experience is vital.

I've seen how this works at Grameen Bank. The bank's board members have respect for and trust in the bank's management; they take advice from the management in making their policy decisions. At the same time, the bank's managers are ready to carry out the wishes of the board. My experience suggests that it is important to provide the board members with the information and skills they need, presented in language they can understand, to make them full partners in designing policies and projects. This includes basic information about financial statements, the fundamental principles of engineering and planning, and data about the economic and other parameters of a plan. Once this is done, the quality of the decisions made by the board members is generally very high.

Yes, it takes a bit of time and energy to empower a team of poor people in this way. But the benefits far outweigh the costs. There are far too many instances of government programs designed without input from the intended beneficiaries that have failed to meet the real needs of the people—and instead have served mainly to line the pockets of politically connected contractors. I'm certain that infrastructure projects designed with the help of poor people will do a much better job of improving the lives of the poor—and will do so at lower cost and with greater efficiency than the kinds of bloated projects typically created by experts with little first-hand understanding of the problems that poor people face.

Making quality education and health care available to all people as an essential element of economic development. The kinds of infrastructure that stimulate economic growth and make it easier for poor people to lift themselves out of poverty aren't limited to roads, bridges, airports, and the like. They also include *human infrastructure*—projects that help to increase the value and creativity of individual lives. That's why, when discussing the need for government-supported infrastructure to help improve and reform the economy, we must talk about the importance of providing education and health care for all people.

Here, as with other kinds of infrastructure programs, social business can play an important role. Elsewhere in this book, I have discussed some of the education and health care programs that the Grameen family of companies has launched. This is not to argue that government should be completely replaced by the citizen sector. Government must provide basic education and health care services. Citizen initiatives can fill the gaps whenever government programs are missing or of poor quality, serving as a backup for government services or as a challenge to them, demonstrating that government has no excuse for its failure to provide the service.

In other cases, government officials may choose to outsource the provision of basic health service and education to organizations from the citizens' sector. When this happens, government should provide necessary supports that will make the work of the citizens' sector more effective and efficient. For example, government can provide investment funds for social businesses focused on education or health care. It can also create separate social business funds dedicated to education and health care projects.

Governments also need to establish basic standards of quality, inclusiveness, and transparency that independent educational and health care organizations must meet. When it comes to profit-seeking private businesses operating in the education and health care sectors, government has to be careful that they do not focus exclusively on extracting profits while ignoring the quality of the services they provide.

Making banking and other financial services available to all. Government has to ensure access to another form of social infrastructure that is vital for the bottom half of people, both men and women—namely, financial services. This is an overlooked form of social infrastructure, perhaps because conventional thinking has never understood the role of financial services in poor people's lives. Financial services like credit, savings, insurance, investment funds, and pension funds create economic opportunity for people and ensure growth at all levels, which is why it's vitally important for government to ensure that such services are available to everybody.

Of course, the story of Grameen Bank vividly illustrates the power of making financial services available to all, especially to poor women who were never on the radar of traditional profit-maximizing banks. Grameen Bank is self-sustaining, runs with its own resources, has a high rate of loan recovery, and is owned mostly by poor female borrowers. It promotes savings; provides insurance and pension fund services; facilitates entrepreneurship; and gives power, freedom, and dignity to millions of illiterate rural women. Grameen Bank's forty-year history of nonstop success helps to explain why the bank won the Nobel Peace Prize back in 2006.

Given this track record, it is surprising that the governments and central banks of the world have largely ignored their responsibility to ensure that the poor have access to financial services. I am disappointed that global women's organizations have not adopted guaranteeing such services as a key item in their agendas for empowering women. Even more shocking is the way Grameen Bank is under attack by the government of Bangladesh. The governing law of Grameen Bank has been amended to convert Grameen Bank into a government-run bank, taking control away from the borrower-owners. The government has not even allowed the bank to appoint its own CEO six years after I was ousted from this position in March 2011.

The things that are happening to Grameen Bank represent a big step backward for the world. Given the history of government-run banks in Bangladesh, one can easily conclude that Grameen Bank is now on a path to disaster. It is heartbreaking to see a history-making, Nobel Prize–winning institution that gave birth to the concept and practice of banking for the poor and inspired the whole world to find a new direction in banking being pushed to take a sharp reverse turn because of these drastic changes in its governing law. The only way to save the bank is to undo the changes. I hope that good sense will prevail before it is too late.

Developing and enforcing fair rules to protect the environment. Another important role for good governance lies in the area of environmental protection. Free, fair markets alone cannot prevent businesses and other organizations—including government agencies themselves—from polluting the air and water, wasting natural resources, and making the catastrophic problem of global climate change even worse.

The well-known dilemma called the *tragedy of the commons* explains why. Environmental protection is a case in which individual interests and group interests sharply diverge. Any single person or organization—a for-profit company, let's say—may benefit from hurting the environment: by cutting corners on carbon emission rules, for example, or by catching an excessive supply of an endangered fish, using plastic in packaging and other consumer products like straws and water bottles, and so on. But if everyone practices the same self-serving behavior, in time the shared good (the commons) will be destroyed, ultimately harming everyone.

In cases like this, an outside force that is greater than any single player and that speaks on behalf of the entire community must step in. Most typically, that force is the government. For the sake of future generations, governments around the world must shoulder the responsibility of establishing and enforcing fair, scientifically sound regulations to protect the air, the water, the soil, and the natural resources on which human life depends.

Strengthening civil institutions that promote human freedoms. I've been arguing that the capitalist system as we know it is harmful without a new sector—the social business sector—that is dedicated to solving the problems we are piling up around us. It is driven by a largely overlooked factor in human behavior: the drive to solve human problems unselfishly for the simple joy and pride that it brings.

Along the same line of reasoning, I argue that our view of society is incomplete and tilted to the disadvantage of the majority of people, if we think merely in terms of government, personal-profit-seeking business, and citizens, all trying to function in accordance with the agreed principles that make up a country's constitution. In this scheme, an important force is missing, one that is essential for the whole system to work in a balanced way. That force is social business, which is created mainly by citizens for the sole purpose of solving the problems created by the profit-driven business sector. Citizens can create social businesses individually, collectively, jointly with other social businesses or profit-driven businesses, with government, or with nonprofit organizations.

Government and profit-driven businesses can also create social businesses.

Civil institutions also play an important role in complementing the other key elements in society. They take many forms. In the United States, for example, civil institutions include political think tanks, lobbying groups, and citizens' organizations; NGOs dedicated to causes like the environment, civil rights, education, health care, and so on; professional organizations and labor unions; foundations and charities; consumer groups; and many others.

These civil institutions play an enormous role in making governments and societies responsive to the needs and wishes of the citizens. They advocate for important legal and legislative changes; they spread vital information; they defend the interests of specific groups within society when those interests are threatened; they represent varying points of view that might otherwise be ignored; and they expose wrongdoing by government officials, business leaders, and other people in power. An extensive network of free, strong, and active civil institutions does a lot to make both good governance and human rights possible.

Unfortunately, in many societies, civil society is not as free, strong, and active as it should be. Governments sometimes use their powers to harass, restrain, and make physical threats against civil institutions. Intelligence agencies may be employed to make it impossible for leading people and organizations from the world of civil society to function. Court cases may be lodged on cooked-up allegations designed to shut down civil institutions that challenge the government, and political organizations may mobilize their members to intimidate or attack civil society leaders whose views they oppose. Over time, common citizens who feel threatened by these assaults simply become silent spectators or play along with the oppressors, feeling helpless to do otherwise.

If we want a society in which human rights are respected and defended, we must recognize the importance of civil institutions and defend them against attack. What's more, we should insist that governments not only refrain from undermining civil society but institute rules and policies that strengthen and nurture it.

Governments that fulfill all of these vital roles—supporting essential infrastructure projects while minimizing corruption and waste and involving poor people in developing plans for such projects; ensuring that basic needs for education, health care, and financial services are being met for all people, including the poor; ensuring an independent judiciary, rule of law, and freedom of the press, and protecting the environment for future generations—such governments can truly be described as well run. If the citizens of the world demand such good governance in every nation on Earth, we will take a big step toward creating the kind of world in which a new economic system beneficial to all people will be possible.

RESPECTING HUMAN RIGHTS: ECONOMIC FREEDOM AND ALL OTHER FREEDOMS ARE LINKED

THERE IS AN INTIMATE CONNECTION between the need for good governance and the defense of human rights. History shows that in the long run, you can't have one without the other. And the same history also affirms that sustainable economic growth that benefits all the people of a society rather than channeling wealth and privilege into the hands of a fortunate few depends on both. Freedom and the elimination of poverty go hand in hand. Human civilization will eventually achieve both—or enjoy neither.

Historical forces, combined with human shortsightedness, fear, and greed, have led to a situation in which most societies have groups that are relegated to the fringes, either through explicit laws and policies or through subtle practices of discrimination and prejudice. Disfavored racial groups, members of specific religions, people who support the wrong political parties, and, above all, the poor—in almost every society there are millions of people whose innate talents and energies are given no chance to flourish.

Over the long arc of history, progress has been made. South African apartheid was abolished; the abuses of Jim Crow in the American South have largely been eliminated; the worst practices associated with the Indian caste system are being tamed. But the commitment to freedom around the world unfortunately ebbs and flows. In 2017, we see troubling signs of backlash against the movement to free and empower all people. Right-wing nationalist groups that demonize racial and ethnic minorities, immigrants, and refugees are growing in popularity in many countries. The trend toward giving equal rights to women and to those with differing sexual orientations is getting pushback from some who claim religious sanction for their views.

Economic freedom and growth are inextricably bound up with human rights and respect for all people. If you want an economic system that liberates human creativity, reduces inequality, and enables everyone to pursue their dreams of a better world, you must defend the rights of all against those who would limit them.

When working men and women want to quit their jobs or when they are asked to quit because of crossing an age limit, they should have the power and opportunity to begin the second phase of their lives—the freedom phase. Society should make this possible by providing social business venture capital that will enable them to become independent entrepreneurs and bring out their creative powers.

I've been emphasizing the importance of liberating young people from the myth that says that their lives and their happiness are dependent on the desires and plans of companies or of a few special individuals known as entrepreneurs. According to this myth, these unique people are "job creators" who produce growth and prosperity single-handedly, through their creativity and brilliance.

I believe that there is no special group of people called entrepreneurs. Everyone is a potential entrepreneur, and all young people should be facilitated to pursue this path. We can all be entrepreneurs, and in so doing we can make the world—and the economy—blossom as never before.

But as successful businesses grow, whether they are social businesses or traditional profit-maximizing companies, they need employees. And if our economic system is to be a fair, free, and equal system that liberates the potential of all people to help make the world a better place, then the rights of employees must also be respected and protected—at least until the day when all employees are also partners in the businesses they work for. So let's guarantee to the working people who choose to remain employees the freedom to organize themselves; the freedom of speech, assembly, and access to the press; and the freedom to vote, so they can demand such basic rights as fair wages, safe working conditions, opportunities for advancement, and control of their own destinies.

Everyone understands that tyranny by government is bad. When government crushes dissent and violates the rights of citizens, an atmosphere of fear is created that stifles creativity, fosters suspicion, and fuels hatred. Societies built on repression are never successful in the long run.

However, the problem of tyranny by a narrow-minded, all-powerful economic system can be almost as bad. When people are afraid to speak their minds because they don't want to offend their bosses and possibly lose the jobs on which their livelihoods depend, then creativity shrivels up.

Writers and artists dependent on for-profit media become timid. Corporations use the power of political donations to bend government policies and rules to their will. Laws and regulations end up being changed to suit the preferences of business leaders. The power that goes with wealth inevitably becomes more and more concentrated in the hands of a few.

Business leaders need to recognize their responsibilities to society and respect the importance of public opinion when formulating their policies. More and more business leaders are feeling the need to reformulate the concept of business by freeing it from the narrow perspective of personal profit. Some of them are embracing a broader concept of business that is based on three equal objectives—people, planet, and profit—rather than profit alone. Until this concept becomes universal, tension will continue to build among businesses, people, and the planet. Citizens' groups will need to continue to protest corporate practices that damage the environment, harm less-powerful communities, or exploit workers.

Business leaders will have to respond to these pressures either willingly or through confrontation. Otherwise, in the long run, they will pay a heavy price for the resentment and hatred their selfish behavior creates, whether through government action or through an uprising by enraged citizens.

• • •

THE TRANSFORMED ECONOMIC SYSTEM THAT is the subject of this book requires significant changes at many levels, from our schools and colleges to our business infrastructure, from the financial system to the laws governing corporations. Some of the changes that need to happen have already begun, as the stories I've recounted illustrate. But the transformation will come to full fruition only when the people of the world demand it and insist that their leaders support it—which includes a commitment to the kinds of good governance practices and human rights protections I've outlined in this chapter.

If anybody tells you that these issues have nothing to do with economics, ignore them. They have everything to do with economics, because they are inextricably tied up with the freedom of humans to express their innate creativity in any form it may take. When everyone has the ability to contribute to the well-being of all, then the world of three zeros that millions of us are already working to create will be one giant step closer to reality.

PART
•••
FOUR

STEPPING STONES TO THE FUTURE

10

THE LEGAL
AND FINANCIAL
INFRASTRUCTURE
WE NEED

THROUGHOUT THIS BOOK, I HAVE been emphasizing the role of individual people—entrepreneurs, housewives, young people, business leaders, community activists, scholars, teachers—in creating the new economic system our world so desperately needs. I strongly believe that each of us has the power to remake society. The first, most important, and perhaps most difficult step is transforming our thinking so that we escape the narrow mental boxes that have constrained the ways we behave.

At the same time, however, the capitalist system does not operate in a vacuum. A framework of laws and institutions makes free markets possible. This includes a legal system that upholds the power of contracts, provides recourse against fraud and exploitation, and defends the rights of all people to decent working conditions, fair wages, and opportunity for advancement. It includes a government that channels a portion of the national wealth to build infrastructure, educate young people, protect the environment, safeguard public health, and defend the country against enemies internal and external. And it includes a financial system that provides sound money as a reliable medium of exchange; makes basic banking, insurance, investment, and other services available to all people; and establishes sources of credit that facilitate the founding and growth of businesses.

All of these are important in helping the world to achieve its many layers of success. But I cannot resist pointing my finger at its massive failures for one simple reason—its misinterpretation of human beings on two counts. First, it assumes that human beings are driven only by their selfishness. Second, it regards human beings primarily as job seekers. If human beings are interpreted in a broader way that is closer to reality, we get a transformed economic system that I am trying to elaborate in this book.

I am not suggesting that we simply discard a system that has helped to produce technological breakthroughs, enormous wealth, and a steady though unequal improvement in the standard of living enjoyed by human beings around the world. Instead, I want to expand the system by replacing today's optionless, one-size-fits-all business world with a world that provides two types of businesses for people to choose from, thereby fully utilizing all the market forces at work in society. Of course, the two types of businesses I am referring to are traditional, profit-maximizing businesses and social businesses that aim to maximize the benefits created for all human beings. And I want to expand our career options by recognizing the fact that all people have the potential to be entrepreneurs—that they can create their own work opportunities rather than relying on someone else to offer them a job.

People should be free to choose from this expanded menu of options or to mix them as they wish. They can choose one, choose the other, or choose both. The system I am proposing is not an imposition on anybody. If people do not choose the new options, the world can stay with the existing system. But if more and more people choose the new options, we have a tremendous chance of creating a different world—the kind of world that we all dream of creating.

What are the implications of introducing social business and universal entrepreneurship within the theoretical framework of economics? It immediately creates the need for changes in every aspect of our economic system. In this chapter, I'll sketch some of the ways our legal and financial framework needs to change, expand, and broaden to accommodate the urgent reforms required to meet today's massive social challenges. As I'll explain, some of the needed changes are already under way. But there is a lot we need to do to support and accelerate them.

Problems with the Existing Legal and Financial Systems

There is no better time than now for a serious discussion of the reforms we need to make in the legal and financial systems that have developed in the wealthy nations of the world.[1] Just a few years ago, in 2008–2009, the world experienced a severe economic crisis that caused incredible hardship for hundreds of millions of people. That crisis originated with problems in the legal and financial systems of the nation that many people consider the most advanced and sophisticated in history—the United States.

During the crisis, a number of highly regulated banks in the United States experienced huge losses and, in some cases, required vast infusions of government funds to avoid complete financial collapse. Enormous sums of public money were used to meet a newly defined public responsibility to protect financial enterprises that were deemed "too big to fail." The problem had many causes, including fraudulent lending practices by some bankers. But most experts agree that the central cause was flaws in the pricing and trading systems used in the markets for mortgage-backed securities and other complex financial instruments devised by the so-called rocket scientists on Wall Street. The complicated interrelationships these instruments created meant that when the weakness of the underlying markets became apparent, panic spread among bankers and investors who realized that they really didn't know what they owned or what its true value was. As a result of the market collapse, millions of ordinary people who had done nothing wrong suffered enormously throughout the world. Many lost their homes, their jobs, and the modest nest eggs they had accumulated through many years of hard work.

Some might consider it ironic that, as the complex financial structures of Wall Street, with their intricate webs of legal safeguards and protections, were collapsing, trust-based microfinance banks like Bangladesh's Grameen Bank continued to flourish, unaffected by the financial uncertainty in the rest of the world. So did Grameen America, the US-based version of microfinance just started in the same year in New York City, the epicenter of the financial crisis. Apparently the integrity and hard work of women living in the villages of Bangladesh and the inner city of New York make a more reliable basis for lasting economic value than the clever constructions of financiers.

A similar situation had occurred in 1997. The macro-economies in a number of Asian countries declined steeply when a bubble of speculative lending burst, but the microfinance organizations in those countries continued to thrive. It seems that during an economic crisis, microfinance organizations can be an island of stability while "mainstream" financial institutions totter.

As I've explained, Grameen Bank issues loans using simple trust-based financial arrangements. No legal documents are involved. We designed a system that is collateral-free—deliberately so, since we intended to reach out to the poor and the poorest. Out of necessity, we built a collateral-free system based on trust and the positive incentives of continued access to credit and other support to ensure loan repayments. Grameen Bank has never used lawyers or courts to collect any of its loans.

In addition, Grameen's business arrangements are simple, straightforward, and transparent. Interest rates for loans and savings are clearly available for all to see on Grameen's website (www.grameen.com). All loans are intended for income-producing activities, housing, and education, not for consumption. The basic interest rate for most business loans is 20 percent on a declining basis, with no compounding; this is below the government-fixed microfinance interest rate of 27 percent. Grameen also has given loans to about one hundred thousand beggars, whom it calls "struggling members." These loans are interest-free and offered without time limits. The goal is to encourage these members to cease begging and to become regular savers and borrowers. A growing number of these borrowers have left begging behind completely and become door-to-door salespeople or adopted other income-generating activities.

The ownership and management structure of Grameen Bank is similarly designed to promote clear lines of accountability and openness. The bank is 75 percent owned by the borrowers (also known as members). Nine of its twelve directors are female borrowers who are elected by their fellow bank borrowers.

The results speak for themselves. Grameen Bank has consistently enjoyed a repayment rate of over 98 percent, even during challenging economic times. The bank is profitable and self-sufficient, generating enough money to remain solvent and independent through its simple system of lending, loan repayments, and member savings. And unlike the mainstream banking system, microcredit has certainly never generated financial uncertainties that have affected the entire society and threatened the stability of the national or world economy.

In view of these facts, one wonders how helpful complex legal contracts have proven to be for the many millions of people and the thousands of institutions involved in the mainstream financial industry. Statistics say that in 50 percent of recent housing foreclosures in the United States, no direct communication existed between the borrower and the lender. By contrast, Grameen's bankers and borrowers meet and look each other in the eye each and every week during the center meetings that are held in eighty thousand villages all over Bangladesh.

Complex contracts that ordinary individuals find impossible to understand do not provide a solid basis for a healthy relationship between bankers and the people they are supposed to serve. It doesn't help matters when the contracts become too complicated even for the bankers themselves to fully understand!

As a partial solution to the failure of contracts to protect the rights of borrowers and other banking customers, government regulators in countries like the United States have created well-intentioned rules mandating disclosure in clear language of the key terms and requirements in any financial agreement. Yet one must ask how successful the disclosure statements are if they are buried in a large pile of documents that are so long and complex that no one seems to fully understand their implications.

I'm not proposing that we should try to radically simplify the legal and financial systems of the developed nations, making them purely trust-based like Grameen Bank. I am saying that the legal and financial challenge of creating a whole new sector of the economy based on selflessness, sharing, and the quest for social benefit—and held together largely by mutual trust rather than formal sanctions—may not be as complex or daunting as you might assume. When you are building an organization whose mission is not to enrich any individual but rather to help make the world a better place for those in need, most people are happy to support it in the same spirit of altruism. Competition among market participants seeking to outwit each other becomes unnecessary. Elaborate safeguards to prevent exploitation are less important than they are in the world of profit-maximizing business.

As long as a clear separation is made between the realm of social business and the realm of traditional profit-maximizing business, both realms will be able to flourish. And as more and more people become familiar with the concept of selfless business, participate in creating social businesses, and enjoy the benefits they create, an understanding of "dog-help-dog" economics will spread. This will make it easier for people to work together in a spirit of mutual trust without the need for elaborate contracts to control their interactions.

HOW THE LEGAL PROFESSION CAN HELP

WHAT MAKES THE TRUST-BASED GRAMEEN model so valuable is that it builds human, family, and social capital by helping the poor—especially poor women—to help each other in a voluntary and businesslike fashion that builds respect, self-esteem, and community. We probably can't apply the same straightforward approach to every economic interaction—at least not yet. But members of the legal profession can begin taking steps today that will help spread the trust-based model to other sectors of society. In this way, they will pave the way for the transformed system of laws that we'll ultimately need to support the new economic system we have begun to build.

Here are some areas for lawyers who share this vision to focus on.

Simplifying laws that govern microfinance programs. I have been advocating for years to create new banking laws to allow the setting up of banks for the poor as opposed to the present laws focused on creating banks for the rich. Doing patchwork on the existing laws to allow noncollateralized lending to the unbanked can have very little success—especially while the need for banking for the unbanked and underbanked is so vast.

I try to present the case by pointing out that financial services are the oxygen of individual economic life. This oxygen is delivered extremely generously to the topmost people; in fact, they enjoy a kind of economic fire that sucks up nearly all the oxygen that is available. In this way the financial system helps cause the extreme concentration of wealth in the world.

Meanwhile, despite the progress that has been made in designing and delivering financial services, the economic oxygen does not reach more than half of the world population. As a result, hundreds of millions live economic lives that are extremely fragile, forcing them to struggle continuously for survival. Provide them with the oxygen, and you'll see how lively and economically healthy they become.

Thus, microcredit is not just about giving tiny loans to poor women. It is a challenge to the entire financial system. Grameen Bank does everything that the traditional bankers used to claim was impossible. It is a simple truth that, if you go by the same road, you'll reach the same destination. If you want to reach a new destination, you'll have to find a new road; if the new road does not exist, you'll have to build it. The road is the means, not the end. In the existing financial system, the road has become the end, while the destination is forgotten.

Everywhere in the world, simpler laws are needed to allow microfinance programs to receive savings deposits from all people and to lend that money to the poor. This can be done by giving limited banking licenses to the NGOs that operate microcredit organizations. In too many jurisdictions, this commonsense practice is not permitted. The right regulations should allow a microfinance organization to expand through mobilizing deposits—the single most important step in expanding microfinance globally.

In the short run, we may not need to wait for the government to pass an entirely new law governing microfinance. While making the best efforts to get a new law, existing laws for various types of financial institutions could be adapted to better support the spread of microcredit and to empower existing facilities. For example, the Reserve Bank of India, the nation's central bank, is now issuing limited banking licenses to successful microfinance institutions run as nonprofit organizations that will allow them to become full-fledged microfinance banks. I have been proposing this simple step to Indian financial authorities for many years, so I am very happy that it is now being done. However, I encourage the authorities to keep sharp eyes on the new microfinance banks, to make sure they don't lose their fundamental character once they get introduced to big money and the bigger opportunities—and temptations—that money creates.

In general, however, the best option would be for national authorities to create new laws exclusively for setting up microfinance banks for low-income people.

Reducing regulations that discourage small-scale entrepreneurship. In the United States in particular, many low-income entrepreneurs find that starting and managing a small business is needlessly difficult because of laws and regulations originally intended or designed for larger businesses. For example, in the State of Louisiana, a person cannot arrange and sell more than one variety of flowers in a vase for resale without taking a test to get a state license.[2] This regulation discourages new entrepreneurs, reduces competition, and keeps the cost of flower arrangements high—just one example of the hundreds of government rules that make it harder for people to start small businesses without creating offsetting benefits. The rules could be changed to make such licensure voluntary and optional, allowing purchasers of flower arrangements to decide whether they want flowers arranged by a licensed or unlicensed business person.

Naturally, it's important to make sure that rules necessary to protect the public, safeguard the environment, and prevent fraud are not weakened. Legislatures should consider empowering ombudsmen or designated commissions to study existing regulations and solicit expert, impartial advice about which ones can and should be eliminated or simplified.

Providing regulatory waivers for the poor. Very poor people engaged in entrepreneurship should be given regulatory waivers entitling them to minimal interference from laws that weren't designed with them in mind. I have seen in many countries—more in rich countries than in poor countries—how regulations make it almost impossible for poor people and young people to enter into business. A waiver program to free them from such regulations could be considered analogous to the free trade or special enterprise zones commonly established to reduce tax burdens in localities where economic need is greatest. In similar fashion, we should create legal interference-free zones where the poor and the young will find it easier to become self-reliant by making a living for themselves. Of course, such programs should not compromise essential rules affecting safety and environmental protection.

Designing welfare and health care laws so that they encourage individual independence. Government programs providing safety-net help for poor people are often poorly designed in ways that encourage dependence rather than independence. For example, they often sharply limit how much money a low-income person can save or earn while still remaining eligible for government assistance with food, housing, or health care. Creative policy changes should be put in place to help people gain self-respect and independence by taking care of themselves through income-producing activities. Subsidies should be phased out in stages rather than all at once when a particular income threshold is reached. This will encourage welfare recipients to take experimental steps to turn into entrepreneurs with the goal of ultimately escaping from welfare.

What about creating tax laws to give special tax privileges to social businesses? Is this a legal step we should take to encourage the spread of this new kind of business?

In the current economic system, social businesses occupy a curious in-between status. They don't clearly fit into either of the two main categories of organizations: for-profit businesses and nonprofit organizations. Like for-profit businesses, they are registered under the business law, have owners, are financially sustainable, have customers who buy goods or services, and return investment capital to investors over time. But like nonprofit organizations, they are solely dedicated to the welfare of people and the planet; they do not seek to maximize profits, nor do they serve the purpose of generating wealth for their owners. They resemble nonprofits in that they seek to serve the greater good—but they do so in a businesslike manner. That creates a big difference between charity and social business. A charity dollar can be used only once, while a social business investment dollar is recycled indefinitely.

In these complicated circumstances, it is argued that since current laws offer tax benefits to charitable organizations, new tax laws are needed to put social businesses on an equal footing with charities. I disagree with this proposal. The main reason is my desire to prevent abuse of social businesses by unscrupulous people who may cleverly hide their personal profit-making in their businesses and present them as social businesses to the authorities in order to claim tax benefits. If such tax exemptions are allowed, I am afraid this may be an open invitation to create false social businesses, leading eventually to a situation where false social businesses will outnumber the genuine ones. Tax officials responsible for deciding which business is a social business will end up with discretionary power, preparing a fertile ground for corruption.

Therefore, to ensure transparency and to protect the integrity of social business, I think it is important that social businesses be covered under the same tax laws as conventional businesses. Social businesses are based on the selflessness of people. Let them be driven by selflessness without being incentivized by tax exemptions.

Simplifying the visa, immigration, and passport systems to encourage international travel. Current systems that restrict the freedom to travel worldwide are a great source of frustration and wasted time and resources. Among those who suffer most as a result of the bureaucratic barriers to travel are poor people and youth—including, for example, young Bangladeshis who want to travel abroad in search of educational opportunities, decent livelihoods, and a better future.

It's interesting to note that until about a hundred years ago, the requirement for visas to cross international borders didn't even exist. When citizens of the great colonial powers moved around the world, they did not need a passport or visa. Visas first became necessary during World War I. After World War II, when the people of Europe launched the grand idea of the European Union (EU), it represented a big step toward returning to the visa-less world of the past, opening up the borders that separate EU countries for free, unfettered travel. We need to accelerate our progress toward a world without visas rather than reversing it.

Recent moves by the US government to make international travel even more difficult will only snuff out one of the few sources of hope enjoyed by deprived people around the world. Closing off yet another source of opportunity will leave the poor people of the world with few options other than bursting out in mass anger. We need to insist on open travel among the nations of the world—an important step on the path toward a world where wealth and opportunity are distributed fairly among all people.

You might notice what all of my legal suggestions have in common. All propose ways to sweep away barriers that prevent people and communities from developing their strengths to the fullest. My fundamental quarrel with mainstream economics is that it imprisons people in a system that holds them back. Those who shape our laws—government officials, attorneys, politicians, community activists, and others—should look closely at the ways the existing economic and legal framework limits the freedom of individuals, especially the poor, to make the most of their innate talents. Hemming poor people in with legal fences and regulatory restrictions has not helped them escape poverty.

Where Will the Money Come From?

One of the most persistent questions I got when I first started to speak about social business was, "Where is the money to fund it going to come from?" Today, with thousands of social businesses under way, funded by corporations, nonprofit organizations, investors, and individual entrepreneurs, it is becoming clearer that many people and institutions are eager to support businesses that aim to solve the most challenging problems human society faces.

Still, the question persists. Sometimes it takes a form like, "Government programs to help the poor are going begging in so many countries these days! How can you get people to provide money for social businesses designed to help those same people?"

The question seems to assume that we live in a world where resources for important needs are difficult to find. But that's false, as a simple glance around you will show. Government budgets are in the hundreds of billions of dollars and steadily climbing. Funds for armies and weaponry flow freely in countries all around the world. Cities on every continent are filled with cranes erecting giant skyscrapers to be occupied by thriving businesses and wealthy individuals. Corporate valuations on the world's stock exchanges keep hitting new highs. Global financial markets are currently awash in an estimated US$210 trillion in investment money, much of it constantly flowing from one temporary home to another in search of even greater growth.

Money is not in short supply. People live in an ocean of money. Only poor people cannot get a sip of it. The world has created a series of bubbles filled with people who ignore what is happening in the lower bubbles. The uppermost bubble is the one where all the wealth is concentrated, while the lowest bubble has the most people and the least wealth. Over time, the uppermost bubble has fewer and fewer people with more and more wealth, making the wealth monopoly more and more extreme.

The reforms to the economic system that I've described in this book aim to change all that. To jump-start these changes, we need to channel a portion of the vast flows of money that already exist throughout the world in a new direction— toward businesses designed to solve the biggest problems of the world, including helping the poor make more productive use of their innate talents and resources. Over time, this re-directed flow will transform the gross imbalance from which we now suffer into a world where greater economic equality reigns, and where everyone will have access to the ocean of money . . . to drink from, and to water the gardens of the future where the right type of growth will sprout.

Grameen Bank was a pioneering effort to divert a small amount of financial water to the poor so that they can start drinking their share and become financially active and creative. With the spread of social business, more financial pipelines are beginning to be created to help to bring money to the people and organizations who are coming forward to solve global problems.

It's not difficult to figure out where the funds for this effort can come from. Here's just one example: We already know the names of the eight people who own more wealth than the bottom half of the world's population, as well as how much wealth each of them has. If those hyperwealthy individuals were to agree to give away half of their wealth for the benefit of the world, the flow of money would immediately change its direction.

I hear you objecting, "How can we persuade those eight people at the top of the pyramid to give away so much of their incredible wealth?" Surprisingly, that's not an issue. We don't need to persuade them. They have already decided to do it! All eight of have signed the Giving Pledge, by which they promise to give away half of their wealth for charity after their death. These eight people are among the many billionaires around the world who have signed the Giving Pledge. (As of mid-2016, the number had surpassed 150, with more signatories continuing to join the list.)[3]

One of the eight wealthiest billionaires is Mark Zuckerberg, the founder and CEO of Facebook. In 2015, when his first child, a daughter named Max, was born, Zuckerberg issued a public statement announcing plans to make a charitable donation of 99 percent of his Facebook shares—the vast bulk of his personal wealth. The statement was accompanied by a filing with the Securities and Exchange Commission making the gift official. What was Zuckerberg's reason for doing this? He gave a clear explanation: he wanted to use his money to help create a better world for his daughter, rather than leaving her a world suffering from terrible human problems.[4]

The existence of the Giving Pledge, and its popularity among the world's wealthiest, is a healthy sign. Now all we have to do is to convince them that at least a portion of this money should be used for social business. If they agree, there will be endless money for all the social businesses we can create in the world. The money so invested will never disappear; instead it will keep on circulating and growing as social businesses expand and multiply. In the meantime, all the other present and future signatories of the pledge may be encouraged to include social business in their commitment.

Here I would like to highlight an important point: one does not have to be a billionaire to make one's own Giving Pledge. Any of us can do that. I would encourage every individual with any means to create his or her own social business trust, putting half or more of his or her wealth into the trust for social business investments during phase two of his or her life (while keeping enough savings to take care of any personal needs). You can remain the CEO of your social business trust as long as you live, and even draw a salary for managing the trust.

People often ask me, "What is the incentive for an individual to put money into a social business or a social business trust?" The answer is simple. Making money is happiness, but making other people happy is super happiness! Once you taste this super happiness, you cannot stop yourself from wanting more.

Every other kind of investment fund in the world can also contribute to the growth of social business. Imagine if all the retirement funds, pension funds, family funds, college endowments, and every other fund made it a policy to invest 1 percent of its assets in a social business trust! Think what that could mean to the world.

Donor countries can also redesign their development aid policies. They can create their own social business trusts or funds in each recipient country and invest at least half of their grant funds into these trusts.

Under the circumstances, how can anyone believe that there is a shortage of money for social business?

Some argue that it is government's job to create organizations that will serve the poor, including microcredit banks to provide them with financial services. I oppose this idea. I would be very careful about using government money for any social business that focuses on lending money to low-income people. For example, I would not recommend that governments get involved in running microcredit banks or programs. It's extremely difficult for a political entity to recover money that it has loaned to poor people. Even when the poor people are willing and able to make repayment—which is usually the case—demanding repayment from them is often politically unpalatable for governments. Citizens are given to believe that government is responsible for taking care of the poor and disadvantaged. This is an obligation of a government. Therefore, when a government agency demands loan repayments from the poor, this seems inconsistent with the responsibilities of government, which makes poor people reluctant to repay funds they've received from a government program. Further-more, since governments are run by politicians, they tend to be more interested in getting votes from the recipients of government money rather than getting the money back. As a result, the important discipline of paying back a loan or investment tends to get lost when a government program is the source.

With the exception of lending programs, governments can often address social problems more efficiently through social businesses than through charity agencies or government-owned commercial enterprises. The essential condition is that each social business should be run as an independent, self-contained business unit, created under the regular company law and controlled only by its board. All staff members should be legally considered employees of the company, not employ-ees of the government. Any profits should either be reinvested in the social business that generates them or invested in other social businesses. Like any other social businesses, social busi-nesses launched through government investments should en-joy the power to expand and reengineer themselves as needed to attain the social objectives for which they were created.

Infrastructure facilities owned by the government could also be designed as social businesses instead of operating them as government agencies. Government-owned factories, busi-nesses, airlines, airports, railways, energy companies, mines, and other basic industries can be designed and operated as social businesses. Governments can create social business joint ventures with private-sector profit-maximizing businesses and with privately owned social businesses.

Government support for the social business structure will yield a number of benefits. As owners of the social businesses, the government agencies that provide the investment funds will get their investment back, saving money for taxpayers. The financial details of each of these social businesses will be made public, assuring citizens that the enterprises are free of corruption and that the social benefits for which the businesses were founded are being generated.

CREATING FINANCIAL STRUCTURES THAT CAN PROMOTE ECONOMIC REFORM

AS I'VE ALREADY SUGGESTED, ONE powerful tool for channeling investment money into social business of all types is the creation of *social business funds.* A social business fund is similar to a conventional profit-oriented investment fund managed by an experienced investment team. The fund managers choose companies to invest in and monitor the results carefully. However, unlike personal profit–seeking investment funds, social business funds focus on social businesses rather than on profit-maximizing companies. Since a social business fund cannot take any profit from its funded enterprises, it has to charge a service fee from the enterprises to cover its cost. However, its goal is not to invest in companies that promise to generate big profits but rather to support companies that are generating big social benefits—reducing poverty, improving nutrition, providing health care, and so on. Investors in a social business fund benefit from the expertise and the watchful eye of the fund managers, as well as from knowing that their money is supporting a range of social businesses doing various kinds of good in the world.

One of the earliest social business funds was established by Crédit Agricole, an old and distinguished bank in France originally created to serve the needs of farmers through a network of regional and local cooperative banks. Now it is a diversified financial services company that is the largest in France.

Jean-Luc Perron, then a senior executive in charge of European affairs at Crédit Agricole, became interested in microcredit in 2006. He found that Georges Pauget, then the CEO of Crédit Agricole, was also a strong supporter of the idea that the bank should play an active role in promoting microcredit as a tool to eradicate poverty. Perron proposed a plan for action by the bank. As part of the implementation of that plan, Perron and Pauget decided to visit Bangladesh for several days in July 2007 to get an on-the-ground understanding of Grameen Bank and to ask the bank to partner with Crédit Agricole in its initiative.

While in Bangladesh, they traveled through the countryside, witnessed firsthand how Grameen Bank branches operate, and ultimately came to meet me to ask me to help them. They proposed a partnership with Crédit Agricole in supporting microcredit as well as the broader concept of social business.

After working out the ground rules, we agreed to work together on a global scale. As a result, Crédit Agricole launched a foundation jointly with Grameen Trust under the name of Grameen Crédit Agricole Microfinance Foundation (GCA). The goal of the trust was to provide finance to microfinance programs that could not expand their activities because of lack of funds. Crédit Agricole endowed the new foundation with 50 million euros, and Jean-Luc Perron became its managing director.

Today, GCA supports around fifty microfinance programs in twenty-seven countries in the developing world, especially on the continent of Africa. In 2012 the foundation added a new program to support social businesses, which it created as a separate social business fund.

The fund itself is designed as a social business. Its aim is to draw investment money from a number of socially minded investors, including the foundation itself. The fund managers then choose social business companies to invest in, weighing the sustainability of the proposed businesses and the social benefits created. The fund also provides technical assistance to its social business partners.

Perron explains that the fund has moved cautiously, studying potential investments carefully and choosing only the most promising to receive funding. "Investing in social business is more difficult, and a bit more risky, than investing in microcredit," Perron explains. "Microcredit is a well-established financial technology proven through extensive experience. By contrast, every new social business is unique! So we devote a lot of time to working with company founders before deciding whether or not to offer them support."

As of early 2017, the GCA social business fund has invested in fifteen social businesses, which are involved in the health, agriculture, renewable energy, and cultural sectors. Examples include the following:

- Laiterie du Berger, a dairy that collects milk from Fulani herders in northern Senegal and converts it into yogurt and other products sold under the brand name Dolima.
- Green Village Ventures, which provides rural households in Uttar Pradesh, one of the poorest states in India, with access to solar power.
- Phare Performing Social Enterprise, a Cambodian company that operates a big-top circus in Siem Reap

and performs shows inspired by contemporary circus skills as well as the traditional performing arts of Cambodian culture. It employs a troupe of sixty artists from underprivileged families who have been trained by Phare Ponleu Selpak, an NGO dedicated to this purpose.

AMONG OTHER SOCIAL BUSINESSES, GCA also supports Agriculture and Climate Risk Enterprise Ltd. (ACRE), the Africa-based company providing crop insurance to small farmers that I described in Chapter 8.

Danone is another organization that has become involved in funding social businesses. I explained in Chapter 3 how Danone's chairman and then-CEO Franck Riboud became interested in the concept of social business and launched the first joint venture social business—Grameen Danone Foods, which provides nutritious yogurt for poor families in Bangladesh. The shareholders and employees of Danone were so excited about participating in the creation of this new kind of business that Danone decided to take this opportunity to expand its support for social businesses in an institutional way.

The result is Danone Communities, a fund dedicated to investing in social businesses. The shareholders and employees of Danone contributed an initial sum of 65 million euros for the find. Now money continues to flow into the fund from Danone employees as well as from outside investors who want to participate. As currently structured, the fund invests 90 percent of its assets in fixed-income securities (bonds) that generate traditional investment income. The remaining 10 percent is invested in a venture capital fund that supports social businesses. The Danone Communities fund's current investments include the following:

- NutriGo, a company that fights infant malnutrition in China through sales of YingYangBao, a fortified supplement.
- Naandi Community Water Services, which makes safe, affordable drinking water available to poor communities in India.
- Isomir, a French company that creates small food processing plants that can be operated by groups of local farmers, providing an enhanced income for agricultural producers who are otherwise at the margin of sustainability.

Like GCA, the Danone Communities fund provides the companies it supports with expertise and advice, including know-how from the nutrition, production, and marketing experts at Danone.

Other social business funds have been springing up around the world. Each operates in its own way, investing in a selection of social businesses from one or more chosen countries and drawing investment money from individuals or organizations that are eager to participate in the new economy that is now being constructed.

Every social business fund has its own unique background story. Here is one of them:

In 2010, I was addressing a conference in Mumbai, India. Among other things, I explained how social business can get a boost from financing facilities in the shape of a social business fund. While I was leaving the stage, a person I'd never met before stopped me to ask a question. "What would you say should be the minimum size of a social business fund in India?" he asked.

I promptly responded, "It should start with at least a million dollars."

The man nodded and walked alongside me as I headed for the exit from the hotel, asking some other questions about how a social business fund might operate. When I reached the front door, he shook my hand and said, "Good-bye, Professor Yunus, and thank you. I'm going to start a social business fund for India."

I wished him well, but I didn't take him seriously. I thought his plan had been born during a moment of inspiration, and I figured that his enthusiasm might melt in the face of business realities. I suspected it might not survive the challenge of actually having to find the money for the fund.

I was wrong. Within a month, I was dumbfounded to receive a letter from Mr. S. K. Shelgikar, the man I had chatted with in Mumbai. It turned out that he is a finance and investment expert. His letter informed me that a social business fund with $1 million of his own money was ready to be registered in Mumbai. He wanted my permission to call it Yunus Social Business Fund Mumbai. I agreed to this. For the last seven years, the fund has been in operation, supporting local social businesses in Mumbai under Mr. Shelgikar's loving care.

Other social business funds continue to spring up. For example, a Yunus Social Business Fund was established in Bengaluru, India, in 2016. It plans to start by supporting four or five social businesses in sectors like education, health care, housing, and education, with investments from around US$75,000 each. It was launched by Vinatha Reddy, who founded Grameen Koota, a Grameen Bank replication in the early years of microfinance in India, and Suresh Krishna,

CEO of Grameen Koota, using funds from Vinatha's family foundation.

In the United States, the Grameen America Social Business Fund was launched in 2016 with initial financial support from the Sara Blakely Foundation, named after the entrepreneur who created Spanx, Inc. This fund will support female social business entrepreneurs in cities and communities around the United States.

Yunus Social Business has also created social business funds in the countries where it operates. Other social business funds are active or being formed in countries around the world, from Europe and Asia to Latin America and Africa.

Governments can create social business funds of various kinds. For example, a fund could specialize in a particular area of interest, such as the environment, poverty, entrepreneurship, agriculture, or health care. Governments can also create regional or local social business funds to support areas with special needs. Money for these funds can include seed money provided by the government as well as the profits from existing government-owned social businesses, recycled to support new social businesses.

Donor countries that support global development can create a social business fund in each country where they operate by donating a part of their grant money. The fund can invest in priority areas chosen by the donor. Each social business created will have its own sustainable life, while donor money will come back to the fund to get invested many times more in the future, rather than disappearing after onetime use, as is the case with charity. Donors can encourage local companies and international corporations—particularly those headquartered in their own countries—to create joint venture social businesses with the fund. Companies can also help to expand the capacity of the fund by providing experience, management skills, and technology.

Social business funds aren't the only new form of funding that innovators are developing to promote change in the global economy. A number of other experiments are under way that illustrate both the significant demand for social business funding and the creative possibilities that exist for channeling some of the world's vast financial resources into this vibrant, rapidly growing sector.

One example is the Social Success Note. This is an ingenious new structure for financing social business that has recently been developed by a team of innovative financial instrument designers from Yunus Social Business (YSB) and the Rockefeller Foundation. The Social Success Note can be viewed as a variation on the financing mechanism known as *results-based financing*. In this system, a government agency or a charity organization underwrites loans from private investors to a nonprofit organization that wants to start a project to pursue some specified social goal. If the program created by the nonprofit meets agreed performance targets, the government will provide funds that make possible bondlike return on the loans. This strategy has been used successfully to attract funding for social programs from private investors like Goldman Sachs.

The Social Success Note offers a new twist on this approach. It involves teamwork among three participants: a social business, an investor, and a philanthropic donor, such as a foundation. The investor provides funding in the form of a loan to the social business to pursue a particular, well-defined social goal—building homes for a certain number of homeless people, for example, or extending health insurance to a certain number of families. The social business is responsible for repaying the loan. But if it achieves the predetermined goal by an agreed deadline, the philanthropic donor will add on an *impact payment* to the investor.

As I noted in an article in *Bloomberg View,* the Social Success Note creates a "win-win-win" scenario:

> Investors receive a risk-adjusted commercial return, thanks to the impact payment; foundations achieve far greater leverage for their philanthropic dollars while achieving a desired social outcome; and social businesses receive access to low-cost capital, allowing them to focus on improving the world without the pressure of offering market-rate financial returns.[5]

THE SOCIAL SUCCESS NOTE REPRESENTS a clever way of aligning incentives among three interested parties so as to encourage the flow of investment money toward projects that will benefit humankind. As companies begin to experiment with this new form of financing, further innovative variations will surely be created. Time will tell which financial mechanisms will prove to be most successful in driving the future growth of the social business sector.

In the long run, the financing tools I've described in this chapter will probably turn out to be temporary, stopgap measures. One day, I believe, there will be social business banks, social business brokerage firms, and social business venture capital funds that will provide funding for the social business sector routinely.

• • •

THE HARDEST PART ABOUT CREATING a new economic system is building up the initial momentum behind change.

That's the effort we are now mounting. Introducing reforms to the world's legal and financial systems is part of the effort. Each reform removes some of the barriers that currently discourage creative experimentation with economic change.

In the years to come, as the successes of social businesses continue to multiply and expand, more and more people and organizations will join the cause. Eventually, we'll wonder why it took so long for the world to recognize the obvious demand for an economic system that is truly dedicated to meeting human needs.

11

REDESIGNING THE WORLD
OF TOMORROW

T HE CONCEPTUAL FRAMEWORK OF CAPITALISM was
originally laid out by the great Scottish economist and
philosopher Adam Smith, primarily in his 1776 book *An In-
quiry into the Nature and Causes of the Wealth of Nations.* This
framework has been improved and elaborated throughout its
long history, but the basic tenets have remained unchanged.
Over time, many alternatives to capitalism have been offered
and practiced. In the meantime, the world has changed enormously. The need for reviewing and reevaluating the basic
structure of capitalism has been felt on many occasions. But it
has never been felt as strongly as it is being felt today.

The world is in serious crisis. I join millions of other people in feeling that capitalism is the root cause of this crisis.
Very few people are calling for it to be abandoned in favor of
some other system, such as socialism, because nearly everyone
is convinced that, with all its faults, capitalism is still a better economic system. Yet in light of the current crisis, there is
strong support for a major overhaul of the system.

In this book, I've explained why I think certain fundamental changes in the theoretical and practical framework of
capitalism are necessary—changes that will allow individuals
to express themselves in multidimensional ways and address
the problems left unsolved or even exacerbated by the existing
conceptual framework. And although my proposal may be
viewed as a significant change in the structure of capitalism, I
see no option but to address these basic flaws in the structure.

In my view, the theoretical framework of capitalism that
is widely accepted today is a half-built structure—one that
turns Adam Smith's "invisible hand" into a heavily biased
hand that pushes the activities of the market in favor of the
richest. One might almost suspect that the "invisible hand"
actually belongs to the richest!

As I've discussed, the present theory of capitalism holds
that the marketplace is reserved for those who are interested
in profit only—an interpretation that treats people as one-
dimensional beings. But people are multidimensional. While
humans have their selfish dimension, they also have their
selfless dimension. The theory of capitalism and the marketplace that has grown up around it makes no room for the
selfless dimension of people. My proposal for change is built
around reinterpreting capitalism by introducing a new view
of humankind—one that is closer to a Real Person than the
Capitalist Man of current theory. This makes a gulf of difference in our concepts, in our practices, and in the institutional
framework of economics. I've argued in this book that if the
altruistic motivation that exists in all people could be brought
into the business world, there would be few problems that we
could not solve.

Adam Smith saw this clearly two and a half centuries ago.
His 1759 book, *The Theory of Moral Sentiments,* begins this
way:

How selfish soever man may be supposed, there are evidently some principles in his nature, which interest him in the fortune of others, and render their happiness necessary to him, though he derives nothing from it except the pleasure of seeing it. Of this kind is pity or compassion, the emotion which we feel for the misery of others, when we either see it, or are made to conceive it in a very lively manner. That we often derive sorrow from the sorrow of others, is a matter of fact too obvious to require any instances to prove it; for this sentiment, like all the other original passions of human nature, is by no means confined to the virtuous and humane, though they perhaps may feel it with the most exquisite sensibility. The greatest ruffian, the most hardened violator of the laws of society, is not altogether without it.

SMITH THEN ASKS THAT MOST fundamental question: Why do we regard certain actions or intentions with approval and condemn others? At the time, opinion was divided: some held that the only standard of right and wrong was the law and the sovereign who made it; others held that moral principles could be worked out rationally, like the theorems of mathematics.

Smith took the view that people are born with a moral sense, just as they have inborn ideas of beauty and harmony. Our conscience tells us what is right and wrong, and that conscience is something innate, not something given to us by lawmakers or derived from rational analysis. And to bolster it we also have a natural fellow-feeling, which Smith calls *sympathy*. Between them, these natural senses of conscience and sympathy ensure that human beings can and do live together in orderly and beneficial social organizations.

Smith's other great book, *The Wealth of Nations,* departed completely from his thesis on moral sentiments. His thesis in *The Wealth of Nations* is generally summarized as an argument that all will be well if people are allowed to follow "self-interest." Whatever Smith had in mind in using the word *self-interest,* the world has interpreted it as equivalent to profit maximization. In effect, self-interest is viewed as the same as selfishness. As a result, the world beyond self has largely faded away from the business mind.

In *The Theory of Moral Sentiments,* Smith elaborated on the great importance of justice and other moral virtues. But he never reconciled this with the concept of self-interest on which *The Wealth of Nations* is anchored. If he had used his two books to propose theoretical foundations for two different types of businesses, perhaps the world could have avoided the serious crisis we are facing today.

The present structure of economic theory does not allow the selfless dimension of people to play out in a marketplace dedicated solely to self-interest-driven businesses. As I've shown in this book, given the opportunity, people will come into the marketplace to express their selfless urges by running businesses specifically designed to improve the lot of humanity in general—a clear improvement on the work of charities. Charitable efforts have always been with us. They are noble, and they are needed. But business has a greater ability than charity to innovate, to expand, and to reach more and more people through the power of the free market. There's no limit to what we can achieve if talented entrepreneurs and business leaders around the world devote themselves to goals such as ending malnutrition and unemployment, creating shelter for the homeless, and providing renewable energy and decent health care to all.

Capitalism in Crisis

With the world's population approaching 8 billion people, it is more crucial than ever that we reevaluate the concept of capitalism. Will we continue to sacrifice the environment, our health, and our children's future in the relentless pursuit of money and power? Or will we take the destiny of the planet into our hands by reimagining a world where we put the needs of all people at the center, and where our creativity, wealth, and other resources become a means to achieve those needs?

Rethinking and remaking our economic system is not simply a nice idea. There really is no viable alternative if we hope to enjoy a future on this planet. While short-term trends may appear to benefit a few of us at the expense of many others, in the long run only policies that will allow all the people of the world to share the progress are truly sustainable. The fate of high-net-worth investors served by bankers on Wall Street and that of poor women working in a garment factory in Bangladesh are linked together. The fate of a sorghum farmer in Uganda, a maize farmer in Mexico, and a soybean farmer in Iowa are all intertwined.

Over the past decade, we've seen our world lurch from one crisis to another: financial disasters, famines, energy shortages, environmental catastrophes, military conflicts, floods of refugees, rising political instability. Populist leaders are calling for walls to be built between countries; they are calling for nations to suddenly abandon international unions built over decades of dedicated diplomacy and high hopes for shared peace and prosperity. This is the time to bring the world together to face this series of crises in a well-planned, well-managed way—to seize the moment as our best opportunity to design and put in place a new economic and financial architecture so that these types of crises will never occur again, long-standing global problems will be addressed decisively, and the incoherence and deficiencies of the current economic and social order will finally be repaired.

The most important feature of this new global economic architecture will be to bring the half-built theoretical framework of capitalism to completion by incorporating the second type of business, social business, and by reworking the theory to recognize that all human beings are entrepreneurs, not merely providers of labor as present theory assumes. Once these changes are included in the framework, they can play an important role in solving the financial crisis, the food crisis, the energy crisis, and the environmental crisis. The new economic structure will provide the most effective institutional mechanism for addressing the unresolved problems of poverty and disease. Social business can address all the problems that are left behind by the profit-making businesses while correcting their excesses.

The Highest Form of Human Creativity

Social business isn't just an essential tool for resolving the crises that humankind faces. It also represents a wonderful expression of human creativity—perhaps the highest form of creativity that humans are capable of.

We know that the objective of a social business is to meet human needs. But when we are creating a social business, the needs to be met must be defined precisely, because the entire business will be designed according to this objective. This is not a problem in conventional business, because, in a fundamental sense, the objective of every conventional business is the same—to achieve the highest return on investment. Not so in social business. The concrete objective varies from business to business. That's why defining that objective clearly is so important.

Then comes the design of the business. This has to be appropriate to achieve the objective. And because the concrete objectives of social businesses vary so widely, social business design calls forth enormous creative power. In most cases, a social business designer is envisioning something that has never existed before. The task demands a lot of creativity, and that's why it is so exciting.

My own experiences have shown me that once you are successful as a social business designer, you don't want to quit. Once you are bitten by the social business bug, you find yourself wanting to design another business even more powerful than the one you designed before . . . and then another, and another.

Social business is a powerful avenue for self-discovery, self-exploration, and self-definition. Best of all, seeing the social benefits created by the business—the hungry children fed, the homeless families given shelter, the diseased people cured—offers a profound inner satisfaction that no other creative endeavor can match. Believe me, nothing in life is more rewarding than fulfilling the creative passion through the act of imagining a social business and then translating it into reality.

Let every young person grow up knowing that he or she can enter the working world as a creative entrepreneur. Let them get ready every day, thinking about what they will do as adults that will let them take care of their families and make a big difference in the world at the same time. Many boys and girls will fall in love and build a life with their partner because they have the same purpose for their lives and believe in the same goals for the world. They can go on to develop a social business together, creating a family life filled with satisfaction and joy at the same time as they bring greater happiness to the whole world.

• • •

WE ARE FORTUNATE ENOUGH TO have been born in an age of great possibilities—an age of amazing technologies, of great wealth, and of limitless human potential. Now the solutions to many of our world's pressing problems—including problems like hunger, poverty, and disease that have plagued humankind since before the dawn of history—are within reach. Most of these solutions could be accelerated through the creation of a new economic order that includes the powerful tool of social business.

In a world that seems to be creating more and more depressing news every day, we can create an outburst of hope, demonstrating that the indomitable human spirit need never yield to frustration and despair. The purpose of human life on this planet is not merely to survive but to live on it with grace, beauty, and happiness. It is up to us to make it happen. We can create a new civilization based not on greed but on the full range of human values. Let's begin today.

NOTES

CHAPTER 1

1. Annie Lowrey, "Is It Better to Be Poor in Bangladesh or the Mississippi Delta?" *The Atlantic,* March 8, 2017, https://www.the atlantic.com/business/archive/2017/03/angus-deaton-qa/518880/.

2. "Just 8 Men Own Same Wealth as Half the World," Oxfam International, January 16, 2017, https://www.oxfam.org/en/pressroom /pressreleases/2017–01–16/just-8-men-own-same-wealth-half-world.

3. Lauren Carroll and Tom Kertscher, "At DNC, Bernie Sanders Repeats Claim That Top One-Tenth of 1% Owns as Much Wealth as Bottom 90%," Politico, July 26, 2016, http://www .politifact.com/truth-o-meter/statements/2016/jul/26/bernie-s /dnc-bernie-sanders-repeats-claim-top-one-tenth-1-o/.

4. Sean Gorman, "Bernie Sanders Says Walmart Heirs Are Wealthier Than Bottom 40 Percent of Americans," Politico, March 14, 2016, http://www.politifact.com/virginia/statements/2016/mar/14 /bernie-s/bernie-sanders-says-walmart-heirs-are-wealthier-bo/.

5. A number of experiments in developing new, better ways to measure economic growth are already under way. See, for example, Stewart Wallis, "Five Measures of Growth That Are Better Than GDP," World Economic Forum, April 19, 2017, https://www.weforum.org /agenda/2016/04/five-measures-of-growth-that-are-better-than-gdp/.

CHAPTER 2

1. Mark Kinver, "Earth Warming to Climate Tipping Point, Warns Study," BBC News, November 30, 2016, http://www.bbc.com /news/science-environment-38146248.

2. Megan Rowling and Morag MacKinnon, "'No Planet B,' Marchers Worldwide Tell Leaders Before UN Climate Summit," Reuters, November 29, 2015, http://www.reuters.com/article/us -climatechange-summit-demonstrations-idUSKBN0TI00720151129.

CHAPTER 3

1. Rachel Savage, "The Most Entrepreneurial Country in the World Is . . . Uganda?" *Management Today,* June 25, 2015, http://www.managementtoday.co.uk/entrepreneurial-country-world-is-uganda/article/1353317.

2. The following discussion of the food, energy, environmental, and financial crises is adapted in part from Muhammad Yunus, "Adam Smith Lecture at Glasgow University," delivered December 1, 2008, http://www.muhammadyunus.org/index.php/news-media/speeches/210-adam-smith-lecture-at-glasgow-university.

3. "World Food Situation: FAO World Food Price Index," Food and Agriculture Organization of the United Nations, February 2, 2017, http://www.fao.org/worldfoodsituation/foodpricesindex/en/.

4. For example, agriculture policies adopted by the European Union are having a deleterious effect on farmers in Latin America and Africa: see "Making the EU's Common Agricultural Policy Coherent with Development Goals," Overseas Development Institute briefing paper, September 2011, https://www.odi.org/sites/odi.org.uk/files/odi-assets/publications-opinion-files/7279.pdf.

5. Beth Hoffman, "How Increased Meat Consumption in China Changes Landscapes Across the Globe," *Forbes,* March 26, 2014, http://www.forbes.com/sites/bethhoffman/2014/03/26/how-increased-meat-consumption-in-china-changes-landscapes-across-the-globe/#3ba5c62d2443.

6. "Climate Change to Shift Global Spread and Quality of Agricultural Land," Science for Environment Policy, European Commission, February 12, 2015, http://ec.europa.eu/environment/integration/research/newsalert/pdf/climate_change_to_shift_global_spread_quality_agricultural_land_403na1_en.pdf.

7. Sunil Sazawal et al., "Impact of Micronutrient Fortification of Yoghurt on Micronutrient Status Markers and Growth—A Randomized Double Blind Controlled Trial Among School Children in Bangladesh," *BMC Public Health* 2013, 13:514.

8. Simon Parry, "The True Cost of Your Cheap Clothes: Slave Wages for Bangladesh Factory Workers," *Post Magazine,* June 11, 2016, http://www.scmp.com/magazines/post-magazine/article/1970431/true-cost-your-cheap-clothes-slave-wages-bangladesh-factory.

9. For a discussion of the French Action Tank and the social businesses it has helped to launch, see Muhammad Yunus et al., "Reaching the Rich World's Poorest Consumers," *Harvard*

Business Review, March 2015, https://hbr.org/2015/03/reaching-the
-rich-worlds-poorest-consumers.

Chapter 4

1. "Youth Unemployment Rate in Europe (EU Member States) as of December 2016 (Seasonally Adjusted)," Statista: The Statistics Portal, https://www.statista.com/statistics/266228 /youth-unemployment-rate-in-eu-countries/.

2. For example, the U-6 unemployment rate compiled by the US Bureau of Labor Statistics, which includes workers who are "marginally attached" and "discouraged," typically runs about double the U-3 rate that is normally reported in the media: see Kimberly Amadeo, "What Is the Real Unemployment Rate?" The Balance, February 20, 2017, https://www.thebalance.com/what-is-the -real-unemployment-rate-3306198.

3. Gregory Viscusi, "Europe Sacrifices a Generation with 17-Year Unemployment Impasse," Bloomberg, October 7, 2014, http://www .bloomberg.com/news/articles/2014–10–07/europe-sacrifices-a -generation-with-17-year-unemployment-impasse.

4. "Decent Work and the 2030 Agenda for Sustainable Development," International Labour Organization, http://ilo.org/global/topics /sdg-2030/lang—en/index.htm.

5. "Lowering the Recidivism Rate," editorial, *Japan Times,* November 24, 2014, http://www.japantimes.co.jp/opinion/2014/11/24 /editorials/lowering-recidivism-rate/#.WNjw3hjMyqB.

Chapter 5

1. Gardiner Harris, "Borrowed Time on Disappearing Land: Facing Rising Seas, Bangladesh Confronts the Consequences of Climate Change," *New York Times,* March 28, 2014, https://www .nytimes.com/2014/03/29/world/asia/facing-rising-seas-bangladesh -confronts-the-consequences-of-climate-change.html.

2. "About the B Team," http://bteam.org/about/.

Chapter 6

1. United Nations Department of Public Education, "Sustainable Development Goals: 17 Goals to Transform Our World," http:// www.un.org/sustainabledevelopment/sustainable-development-goals/.

2. United Nations Department of Public Education, "Goal 1: End Poverty in All Its Forms Everywhere. Goal 1 Targets," http://www .un.org/sustainabledevelopment/poverty/.

3. Daniel Nowak, "Investing in Social Businesses in the Western Balkans," European Venture Philanthropy Association blog, August 30, 2016, http://evpa.eu.com/blog/investing-in-social-businesses -in-the-western-balkans.

4. Sara Manisera, "She's Helped Change the Prospects of Women Affected by the Bosnian War," *Christian Science Monitor,* September 15, 2016, http://www.csmonitor.com/World/Making-a -difference/2016/0915/She-s-helped-change-the-prospects-of-women -affected-by-the-Bosnian-war.

5. "McCain CE Collaborates to Launch Social Business," McCain website, July 11, 2014, http://www.mccain.com/information-hub/news /some-test-news.

CHAPTER 7

1. Max Ehrenfreund, "A Majority of Millennials Now Reject Capitalism, Poll Shows," *Washington Post,* April 26, 2016, https:// www.washingtonpost.com/news/wonk/wp/2016/04/26/a-majority -of-millennials-now-reject-capitalism-poll-shows/?utm_term= .cb8dbd4baf70.

2. Michael Munger, "Why You Can't Just 'Reject' Capitalism," Learn Liberty, May 15, 2016, http://www.learnliberty.org/blog/why -you-cant-just-reject-capitalism/.

3. Sarah Kendzior, "Why Young Americans Are Giving Up on Capitalism," *Foreign Policy*, June 16, 2016, http://foreignpolicy .com/2016/06/16/why-young-americans-are-giving-up-on-capitalism/.

4. Syeda Nafisa Nawal, "Redefining 'Win-Win': Youth in Social Business," Daily Star [Dhaka, Bangladesh], July 29, 2016, http:// www.thedailystar.net/next-step/youth-social-business-1261174.

5. The following section on old age and retirement is based in part on the keynote address delivered by Muhammad Yunus at the International Federation on Ageing (IFA) 12th Global Ageing Conference in Hyderabad, India, June 10, 2014.

CHAPTER 8

1. Jason Choi, "Emerging Markets Can Be Wildly Profitable— If You Aren't Focused on Mobile and Cloud," *Forbes,* June 8, 2016,

https://www.forbes.com/sites/groupthink/2016/06/08/emerging
-markets-can-be-wildly-profitable-if-you-arent-focused-on-mobile
-and-cloud/#1806387038fe.

2. "How Does MakeSense Work?" MakeSense, November 2015, https://makesense.s3.amazonaws.com/resources/social_entrepreneurs .pdf.

Chapter 9

1. Transparency International Corruption Perceptions Index 2016, January 25, 2017, https://www.transparency.org/news/feature /corruption_perceptions_index_2016.

2. Muhammad Yunus with Karl Weber, *Creating a World Without Poverty* (New York: PublicAffairs, 2007), chap. 5.

Chapter 10

1. The following discussion of legal consideration in reforming the world's economic system is adapted in part from Muhammad Yunus, "How Legal Steps Can Help to Pave the Way to Ending Poverty," *Human Rights Magazine,* Winter 2008, http://www.americanbar .org/publications/human_rights_magazine_home/human_rights _vol35_2008/human_rights_winter2008/hr_winter08_yunus.html.

2. "Retail Florist License," Louisiana Horticulture Commission, http://www.ldaf.state.la.us/consumers/horticulture-programs /louisiana-horticulture-commission/.

3. The Giving Pledge, https://givingpledge.org.

4. Kerry A. Dolan, "Mark Zuckerberg Announces Birth of Baby Girl & Plan to Donate 99% of His Facebook Stock," *Forbes,* December 1, 2015, https://www.forbes.com/sites/kerryadolan/2015/12/01 /mark-zuckerberg-announces-birth-of-baby-girl-plan-to-donate-99 -of-his-facebook-stock/#16d43dc218f5.

5. Muhammad A. Yunus and Judith Rodin, "Save the World, Turn a Profit," *Bloomberg* View, September 25, 2015, https://www .bloomberg.com/view/articles/2015–09–25/save-the-world-turn -a-profit.

INDEX

MUHAMMAD YUNUS, a native of Bangladesh, was educated at Dhaka University and was awarded a Fulbright scholarship to study economics at Vanderbilt University. In 1972 he became head of the economics department at Chittagong University. He is the founder of Grameen Bank and the father of microcredit, an economic movement that has helped lift millions of families around the world out of poverty. He is also the father of social business. Yunus and Grameen Bank are winners of the 2006 Nobel Peace Prize. Yunus Centre Website: http://www.muhammadyunus.org/

PublicAffairs is a publishing house founded in 1997. It is a tribute to the standards, values, and flair of three persons who have served as mentors to countless reporters, writers, editors, and book people of all kinds, including me.

I. F. Stone, proprietor of *I. F. Stone's Weekly*, combined a commitment to the First Amendment with entrepreneurial zeal and reporting skill and became one of the great independent journalists in American history. At the age of eighty, Izzy published *The Trial of Socrates*, which was a national bestseller. He wrote the book after he taught himself ancient Greek.

Benjamin C. Bradlee was for nearly thirty years the charismatic editorial leader of *The Washington Post*. It was Ben who gave the *Post* the range and courage to pursue such historic issues as Watergate. He supported his reporters with a tenacity that made them fearless and it is no accident that so many became authors of influential, best-selling books.

Robert L. Bernstein, the chief executive of Random House for more than a quarter century, guided one of the nation's premier publishing houses. Bob was personally responsible for many books of political dissent and argument that challenged tyranny around the globe. He is also the founder and longtime chair of Human Rights Watch, one of the most respected human rights organizations in the world.

·   ·   ·

For fifty years, the banner of Public Affairs Press was carried by its owner Morris B. Schnapper, who published Gandhi, Nasser, Toynbee, Truman, and about 1,500 other authors. In 1983, Schnapper was described by *The Washington Post* as "a redoubtable gadfly." His legacy will endure in the books to come.

Peter Osnos, *Founder*